MW01131849

COMICS IN WISCONSIN

COMICS in WISCONSIN

BY PAUL BUHLE

Borderland Books

Copyright © 2009 by Paul Buhle

Original illustrations © 2009 by Steve Chappell

All rights reserved. No part of this book may be reproduced in any form without written permission from the publisher, with the exception of brief excerpts for review purposes.

All material is copyrighted by the artists, unless otherwise specified.

Published by Borderland Books, Madison, Wisconsin
www.borderlandbooks.net

Publisher's Cataloging-In-Publication Data
(Prepared by The Donohue Group, Inc.)

Buhle, Paul, 1944-
Comics in Wisconsin / by Paul Buhle.

 p. : ill., map ; cm.

Includes bibliographical references and index.
ISBN: 978-0-9815620-3-2

1. Comic books, strips, etc.--Wisconsin--History. 2. Wisconsin--Politics and government--20th century--Comic books, strips, etc. I. Title.

PN6725 .B84 2009

741.5/9775   2008942234

Printed in the United States of America

Book design by Steve Chappell

ECO-FRIENDLY BOOKS
Made in the USA

CONTENTS

INTRODUCTION

isconsin, a fabled vacationland of the northern Midwest, is too little known for its progressive political traditions and antiwar sentiment and likewise for its contributions to the development of comic art. The centrality of Greater New York and regional outlands for the bulk of comic artists, publishers, and the distributors has been seriously challenged only during the golden years of American journalism, with far-flung newspaper giants and their distinct comics pages, and once again in the late 1960s and much of the 1970s, with production of so-called "underground comix" from the Bay Area. Wisconsin has nevertheless had unique advantages: proximity to Chicago; traditions of free expression, including the counterculture; and radical ideas of history as unvarnished truth-telling.

First came the comic strip, a product of the great daily newspapers, which made comic art commercially viable and raised its profile to the point where a few artists became millionaires as well as household words. Youngsters destined for fame usually displayed their talents locally, then moved on to New York— but not always. The *Chicago Tribune*, famously reactionary until the heroic era of newspapers ended, also happened to be an unlikely fount of hilarious, antic, and rather rebellious comic spirits. Some of the famous strips and artists were far from rebellious, advance agents of the blandness of the funny pages after 1930, but this glum fact does not cancel out the story. Like the Hearst papers and William Randolph Hearst himself, known for antiunionism and a fondness for European fascism, the *Trib* management recognized the popularity of the comic strip and even indulged some great comic artists who were not the most popular among readers.

The Wisconsin comic offers a late twentieth-century counterpart to Chicago comic art as well as an earlier extension. Many a Wisconsin artist must have agreed with native Iowan Floyd Dell's description of the train trip of the aspiring youngster from the outlands to Chicago: the longest ride in the world. Chicago was *their* New York, the global city with opportunities to match. Some artists with real talent for comics stayed behind in Wisconsin.

By the early 1970s, in comics terms, New York had been displaced by Berkeley, and if some Wisconsinians made it there bodily, others set up outposts of the counterculture in Milwaukee, Madison, and points beyond. The Wisconsin role in the transformation of comic art during the 1970s–80s may be idiosyncratic and tied to personal details, but perhaps not. Madison, like Austin, Texas, was itself a metaphor of the period, with all the cultural energies intact, in ways that Seattle would become a fount of alternative culture, music, and comics as the century closed.

An argument can be made that after the turn of the new century, Madison began to sparkle again in comic arts, thanks to a vital heritage as much political as cultural. That argument rests substantially upon the output of nonfiction comics alongside that of a small-scale publishing empire in the Madison exurb of Mount Horeb, and so may strike readers as a conceptual stretch. Still, it's an interesting development, bringing together the story of Wisconsin comic art with Wisconsin progressive politics. It is *our* twist, after all, as recognizable as a fresh cheese curd.

Fabled vacationland of the northern Midwest.

The following pages offer no giant claim but instead, I believe, a narrative and some particular stories of real interest, as well as a lot of fun, not only to Wisconsin readers.

This book could not have been created without the assistance of many people, mainly the publisher, Richard Quinney; after him, the great comics publisher of the 1970s–90s, none other than Denis Kitchen; and a handful of folks who contributed ideas and graphics. My frequent literary collaborator (and fellow German American) Dave Wagner was an editor of a leading underground newspaper in Madison of yore, and his sensitivities for comic art are ever reliable, ever useful. He is also a magnificently talented comics scriptwriter. George Hagenauer supplied details otherwise hopelessly obscure, and pages of *Captain Midnight* to be photographed. Milton Griepp and Bruce Ayres were helpful as always.

Parts of this book have appeared or will appear in issues of *Isthmus* and the *Wisconsin Magazine of History*.

CHAPTER ONE
HOW IT ALL BEGINS

The origins of comic art have been variously traced to the workrooms of the artist-illustrators before the invention of movable type; to the innovators of medieval art, especially Hieronymus Bosch and Pieter Bruegel, for their recognizable ordinary people and their ordinary themes; and to the rise of illustration in nineteenth-century Europe.

The last is the most promising to us, for now, and the literature points directly toward one artist, the distinctly Swiss, radically conservative Rodolphe Töpffer (1799–1846). It is too much to claim him for the Swiss-German Wisconsin mentality, but too tempting not to try. The son of a painter, Töpffer suffered an eye injury in youth and was driven toward lesser art forms not yet invented. When not teaching school or turning out commercial illustrations, Töpffer produced an astonishing quantity of what can only be called comic art. His work, seen all these years later, is humorous only in pain, heavily annotated with description and dialogue (although the dialogue "bubble" had already been invented by caricaturists, he did not employ it) but, with all its limitations, ever lively

The Garden of Earthly Delights, by Hieronymus Bosch, 1503.

and inventive. As biographer David Kunzle notes, Töpffer viewed the forces and details of modernization with extreme dread. Not only militarization but also the spectre of working class revolt and socialism, ostentatious wealth, changing sexual mores, and much more struck the Geneva schoolteacher as the approaching end of decency and perhaps all civilization. If this was progress, he wanted no more of it.

Why do we view Töpffer, rather than such lushly talented caricaturists as Cruikshank and Daumier, as a grandfather of comics? Because of *continuity*, the elaboration of the series of comic panels in which a story is told through a developing narrative. If he was not the only artist to practice continuity, and although he had a fairly low opinion of his own comic work, Töpffer did more, had more recognition (he was the most famous citizen of Geneva, among other things) in his art, than any rivals. It is said that after Töpffer, comic art suffered an apparently calamitous decline until the appearance of comics in the newspaper tabloids of the 1890s, especially in the U.S. The comics reemerged as a vulgar popular art.

That a contemporary critic and devotee of Töpffer describes the artist's contribution as "German" perhaps allows us to slip into the very Germanic Wisconsin of the late nineteenth and early twentieth centuries. With an abundance of fertile farmland and Civil War veterans who had gone south idealistically for the abolition of slavery, Wisconsin saw both the swift rise of capitalism and the

"Blind Man's Bluff," from *Histoire de Monsieur Cryptogame,* by Rodolphe Töpffer, 1830.

unusual (for the U.S.) rise of popular political socialism. Milwaukee was practically a German social democratic city by 1900, and the Wisconsin capital of Madison soon after became the center of a progressive style of government, antimonopolist rhetoric, and eventual opposition to imperial adventure in the form of world war. The best of the opposition to empire was epitomized not in the socialists, not even in their U.S. Representative Victor Berger of Milwaukee, but in the single most admired figure of the state, the progressive governor and U.S. Senator Robert M. La Follette.

Not altogether surprisingly, then, our first comic artists of note are Milwaukee-born T. E. Powers and the better remembered Art Young, whose boyhood was spent in Monroe. Powers (1870–1939) actually spent most of his growing years in Kansas City but attended art school in Chicago and worked first for the *Chicago Daily News* and then Hearst papers, for life. William Randolph Hearst, youthful rebel (but also avid supporter of U.S. military adventures abroad) and newspaper business genius, knew talent when he saw it and encouraged an antimonopoly spirit until his own monopoly over a large part of the daily press was practically complete. Thus, Powers would likely have been encouraged in his early anti-elitist, antimonopolist political cartoons. His sentiments are lightened somewhat in his daily comics, their commentary mainly on morals and manners rather than elections or power-wielding. The characters "Joy" and "Gloom" mark the range of human emotions and outline the sources of human folly. It also might be noted that like early and late comic artists (but few of them during the 1920s–60s), Powers would reveal the illusions of the comic panel limits whenever he chose to speak directly to the reader. It was a way of showing the artist's turn of mind by stripping off the artificial barrier of format.

Art Young (1866–1943) seems to have been a lively teen, his family having relocated from rural Orangeville, Illinois, to Monroe, where he picked up a volume of Gustave Doré illustrations at the public library. His destiny was quickly set, by his own account, in more than one way. Attending art school in Chicago, Young became a promising Republican editorial cartoonist set to tasks such as sketching the condemned anarchist martyrs of the 1886 Haymarket affair. By the turn of the century, he had begun to experience inner doubts and moved toward the Socialist Party of Eugene V. Debs. Young swiftly became the greatest of American socialist comic artists, arguably the best across Europe and the Americas.

"System," by Art Young for the leftist journal *Good Morning*, 1919.

The most extraordinary phase of Young's life may have been time spent among his fellow artists at the *Masses* magazine (1911–17). At once the radical journal of Greenwich Village and the popular expression of the Ash Can artists' circle, it was a highly innovative corner of American culture as well as the voice of the single important art movement in U.S. history. Young, the eldest of the crowd by a generation, stuck it out into the wartime era when the authorities banned the magazine for its antiwar sentiments and threatened to jail its artists and editors. It (and Young) happened to be guilty not only of socialism and antiwar sentiment but

"It Might Have Been Worse!" featuring "Joy" and "Gloom", by T. E. Powers, 1911.

also of support for birth control and feminism. Here, American art met radicalism upon its own ground, a formula for artistic explosion.

The socialist movement was effectively destroyed. Yet it might be said that for Wisconsin and also for the social and cultural climate in most of the rest of the U.S. the energy of the 1910s powered the best of the 1920s. Modern art on this side of the ocean was a pale version of the energy in Paris and elsewhere, and the opening of the Museum of Modern Art actually turned the output of radical avant-garde energy into precious objects. But a kind of hipsterdom was also taking shape. The New York Dadaists, in their dissolution, were fascinated by elements of popular culture, from prize fighters to detective magazines. Surrealists of Europe recognized what the American art crowd ignored or disdained, that the avant-garde had gone underground, hiding in plain sight.

The Masses, cover by Art Young, November 1914.

The Chicago Idea and the Wisconsin Artist

The comic pages as a highly popular section of the daily press solidified during the 1910s–20s. At first the strips were miniature versions of the Sunday funnies, in "gag" format and appearing no more than three times per week. In 1912 Hearst introduced the first daily page of comics, in his *New York Evening Journal*. Four strips daily eventually became nine strips daily. Other newspapers followed suit, and newspaper syndicates quickly assumed control of most strips, distributing them for the artist (and collecting most of the money in the process). It was, as more than one critic has suggested, the television of the 1910s–40s, every bit as popular as contemporary radio, with no layout of cash for hardware among the often impoverished readers. Newspapers competed with each other furiously for new, interesting comics that were "different" narratively and visually, because millions of ordinary readers, rural and urban, often bought a paper for its selection of funnies.

Thus the niche emerged for the comic artist, in most cases a painstaking and highly repetitive daily task without great rewards. For the fortunate (sometimes also brilliantly talented) few, there was a big salary; assistants to do nearly everything, including coming up with fresh ideas; and a life of celebrity nearly as large as any film star's, larger and certainly more beloved than the average White House resident.

From the moment he began starting or buying and redirecting newspapers, Hearst had been collecting comic artists as well. Unlike most other distinguished or college-age Americans, Hearst actually liked comics and was known to keep on those artists whose popularity fell (famously, George Herriman of *Krazy Kat*) because the baron of tabloids had the power and chose simply to do so. Mainly, however, he shrewdly figured out the strips' diverse appeals to the public, recalculating as he went along.

It was Hearst himself who developed the career of Clare Briggs (1875–1930), a Reedsburg native whose parents moved him to several other midwestern locations, all of them presumably providing him sources for the small town Americana that would become his folksy signature. A newspaper sketch artist, then an editorial cartoonist sent off by Hearst to sensationalize the gory U.S. invasion of Cuba, he was next assigned to Chicago and its Hearst paper, the *American*. Briggs created *A. Piker Clerk*, a gag strip about a clerk who continually frustrates seekers with impoliteness and bad information. This strip was, however, merely a phase in Briggs's career, along with lecturing on the vaudeville circuit and animating silent films. He spent seventeen years in Chicago and then moved back to New York. Ironically, his single-panel reflections like *Real Folks at Home* were rural nostalgia served up for big city audiences, although the syndication must have reached far into fading rural memories of more insular days and small town papers.

A. Piker Clerk, by Clare Briggs, 1904. Collection of George Hagenaur.

Second only to Hearst as creator-impresario of the comics was Captain Joseph Medill Patterson, one of the more remarkable characters of twentieth-century American popular culture. A young socialist and playwright in the early 1910s, he changed careers in the second half of the decade, and his cousin Colonel Robert McCormick, owner of the giant *Chicago Tribune*, made him the paper's co-editor in 1917. Even more than Hearst (which is saying something), Patterson intuitively understood the medium, and unlike Hearst, he jumped into the artwork production himself, "coaching" into existence half a dozen of the most popular strips, actually suggesting characters, supplying story lines, and choosing artists from among the paper's staff to graduate into the very big time.

By 1917 or so, Patterson was mulling something that had not yet been done or, at least, firmly established. Continuing characters existed from the first comics (*Mutt and Jeff*, sometime racetrack touts, were the very first to go daily), and readers looked for the protagonists and antagonists who drew their attention. The stories were set around a daily gag that ended with a punch line as a kind of exclamation point (very often the exclamation point itself was featured, perhaps more often than anywhere else in the English language). In Patterson's mind, the lives of average Chicagoans ran more smoothly and more continuously. Thus, "continuity" reentered the comic world, a word that set a new tone for most comic strips (but not all). Inevitably perhaps, the innovation of continuity soon brought on a period of reduced imagination in comics, a blanding of styles and stories. But it suited a deep logic of the newspaper market and the artist making a living there. According to some accounts, Briggs's *A. Piker Clerk* had actually preceded others as a daily strip with a kind of continuity, but it had not made much impact on the comic form. That considerable accomplishment fell to Sidney Smith.

The Sidney Smith story is a popular classic in every sense. Born in 1877 in Bloomington, Illinois, Frank Sidney Smith began contributing cartoons to local papers as a teenager. Going to the commercial metropolis just as a talented Wisconsin youth of his time would, Smith got onto the *Chicago Tribune* staff in 1911 as a sports illustrator. It was Patterson who decided that the comics, interesting as they had become, did not match the lived experience of the average *Tribune* reader: a white and relatively prosperous wage earner or member of the lower-middle class, neither wealthy nor impoverished, a fellow with a family that had the usual problems, from financial disappointments to sibling rivalries, and pleasures, owned a Tin Lizzie, and took a drive to the country on weekends. Thus was the Andy Gump character created. Patterson later recalled that in his childhood days, any loud and boorish adult was called a "gump."

Sidney Smith, who had been turning out a gag strip with animals, *Old Doc Yak*, was picked for this feature and was doubtless happy to reach his destiny. From its February 1917 debut, *The Gumps* rapidly grew in popularity, and so did the paper. The *Tribune* soon came to be known as the "Andy Gump paper," and reputedly rose 35,000 in daily circulation. (In 1923, the Minnesota Board of Trade halted business for an hour to find out if two characters, Andy's millionaire uncle and a gold digger, had got married.) Six years later, Smith killed off a character, something never previously done. An avalanche of angry mail, not all of it ironic, fell upon the paper and the artist.

The Gumps, 1917, by Sidney Smith.

Early in the Roaring Twenties, Smith defected to Lake Geneva, Wisconsin, where he came into his own as a public personality. In 1922, he bought a mansion formerly owned by a close friend and financial supporter of Chicago's famous Hull House settlement and its leader, Jane Addams. Cartoonists still more famous were becoming nightclub and radio personalities in Manhattan, but Smith settled for being a dashing host of what were described as "eccentric parties" in a resort town afloat with oceans of illegal liquor. He was also famous for shuffling three wives in succession and for assorted local gags, like signing dollar bills and giving them away to strangers on the street.

His best gag by far was the Andy Gump campaign for president in 1924. The two major presidential candidates were dull as dishwater and thoroughly conservative, but Robert La Follette of the Progressive Party courageously spoke across the country for farmers' and workers' rights (he carried only Wisconsin). Andy's campaign lasted only one night, at a lawn-party reception at Smith's estate in Lake Geneva, promising to get rid of the railroad monopoly and Wall Street swindlers. (The satire continues to this day: the Andy Gump statue on Wrigley Drive holds the campaign manifesto in its right hand.) La Follette couldn't have put it better. The two candidates, imaginary and real respectively, were cheerful soul brothers.

From there on, Andy Gump only got bigger. Animation, a radio show, a card game, a silent film, and even a Bessie Smith lyric drew upon the Gump legend. The hugely lucrative comic strip "itemization" of assorted gewgaws began here, for better or worse. (Al Capp would soon make it larger in financial terms than his *Li'l Abner* strip itself, completing a pattern.) Ironically, as comics critics observed, the *Gumps* art itself was barely adequate. The story line also tended toward

The Gumps, by Sidney Smith, *Chicago Tribune*, 1924.

lameness, as Andy escaped the tedium or repetition by heading for China's mythic Golden City amid heavy Orientalism (guided by his companion Ching Chow), met conniving male characters threatening to bankrupt him (one succeeds) and female ones threatening to snatch the strip's unwary bachelors, and so on. Still, the masses loved the chinless, increasingly clichéd Andy. Smith's paycheck, for a little while, just happened to be the largest in the comics business: $100,000 per year. He was offered a million bucks and a Rolls-Royce in 1935, but on the way back from Chicago he drove his Ford Sedan smack into another car and died instantly. *The Gumps* didn't leave the papers until 1959, at first because artists always worked ahead of publication and then because the art continued in the hands of a new artist and then another and another.

Joseph Medill Patterson's next creation was the meal ticket of a real homegrown Badger and an extraordinary talent, Frank O. King. Born in 1883 to a banker's daughter and a general store owner in the small town of Tomah, King attended art school in Chicago and joined the same *Tribune* staff as Smith. The two artists, destined to be comic giants of the dailies, worked in close proximity. Patterson had the genius notion of a strip like *The Gumps* built on daily life but more specifically around the automobile craze. King, who had been drawing since high school days for publication and drew a series of forgettable Sunday funnies—the best one, *Bobby Make-Believe*, about a boy's daydream fantasies—for the *Tribune*, now took readers into a new place in American life: Gasoline Alley.

What began in 1918 as a corner of a full-page black-and-white strip, *The*

Bobby Make-Believe, by Frank O. King, 1916.

Rectangle, quickly acquired its own space. Fairly soon, it evolved from a chat session about cars into a more social setting, with occasional women characters on the side. Patterson claimed to have proposed making it a family strip, and he was certainly the boss, but we will never know who moved the concept outward from men's space, greasy overalls, and machinery to something very different. In February 1921, lead character Walt Wallet discovered a foundling child on his doorstep, and most of the gags for a while were about a hapless but loving bachelor seeking to apply mechanical logic and language to caring for a baby. Women now gathered in the panels of the strip, as presumably they did among its readers. Comics scholar Jeet Heer points out that the artist himself had entered a new phase of family life in Chicago's South Side Washington Park, becoming a father in 1916 and moving a few years later to the distinctly upper-class suburb of Glencoe. The strip's famed baby, Skeezix, was only five years younger than King's own boy. Thereafter, lots of father-son adventures, including a family driving trip out West, seemed to be taken from real life.

King was also, of course, inevitably drawing as well upon his own Wisconsin childhood memories, and here is where we may find Tomah and the surrounding Kickapoo Valley set in comic art form. Outside Gasoline Alley the garage, the actual street looks like Tomah's Main Street rather than a Chicago neighborhood,

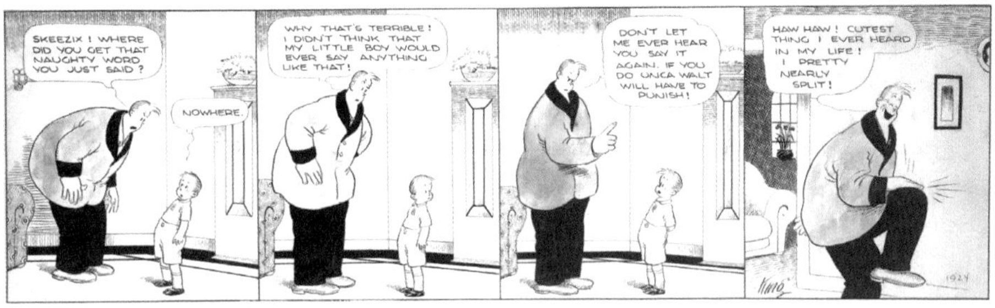
SKEEZIX ! WHERE DID YOU GET THAT NAUGHTY WORD YOU JUST SAID ?
NOWHERE.
WHY THAT'S TERRIBLE ! I DIDN'T THINK THAT MY LITTLE BOY WOULD EVER SAY ANYTHING LIKE THAT !
DON'T LET ME EVER HEAR YOU SAY IT AGAIN. IF YOU DO UNCA WALT WILL HAVE TO PUNISH !
HAW HAW ! CUTEST THING I EVER HEARD IN MY LIFE ! I PRETTY NEARLY SPLIT !
1924

Walt Wallet and Skeezix in *Gasoline Alley*, by Frank O. King, 1924.

and characters have the small-industrial-town feel, although it could have been a lot of other places in contemporary America. The men repaired cars less and less as time went on, while women and the social life of the family became steadily more prominent. The kids, amazingly enough (this was another key innovation, a comic strip first), actually grew bigger and got older, although the adults seemed to age more slowly.

Chris Ware, one of the most admired and visually inventive U.S. comic artists of recent decades, has described King's *Gasoline Alley* this way: "I am convinced that after all these books [i.e., the collected strips] are published, *Gasoline Alley* will stand as one of the most individual, human and genuinely great works in the history of comics." High praise, indeed. Elsewhere, Ware has been quoted as saying that King's contribution to future artists was certainly in visual style and narrative, but more in teaching by example about the way a comic is read and understood by its workaday devotees. Ware's own work frequently gives off a

Gasoline Alley, by Frank O. King, 1930.

sense of distress and nostalgia, as if he would rather live close to Gasoline Alley than anywhere in the twentieth-first century.

Readers, at any rate, loved the family automobile adventures, the give-and-take of parents and children (who seemed to have normal-sized heads and bodies, unlike their parents' small skulls and bulgy bodies), but above all the everydayness, smoother and thus more effective than Smith's. If *Gasoline Alley* might be called the first soap opera, ahead even of network radio, then Walt Wallet and his wife, Phyllis, their adopted son, Skeezix, and assorted other characters were the ones who set the pattern for the teledramas that continue today, for better or worse.

After its lively beginning and early innovations, *Gasoline Alley* displayed limited artistic development, relative to any number of more experimental daily strips of the time. But King's art was actually better than his story line. He had been drawing wild cosmic adventures before accepting the assignment for *Gasoline Alley*, borrowing heavily from early comic strip master Winsor McCay. By 1926, on Sundays with the full palette of color possibilities, King returned to moments of fantasia (and even visual commentary on modern, abstract art) but mostly to a kind of nature lore, experienced by father and son for the most part. It was the kind of art that a man from a small town in Wisconsin, just large enough for commerce and some industry but surrounded by countryside, would see and feel. His artistic experiments with overhead shots, as if from a helicopter or air balloon, were widely enjoyed and have, in recent years, been increasingly admired as proof of comic art's existence. An argument can be made that King was the realist master of the successfully integrated story-and-picture that brought comic art forward. The difficulty of this claim is that the great majority of realist comic art of the 1930s–50s was stylized pseudorealism, much of it a white man's adventure on the street corner, on the battlefield, in the jungle, and in the mysterious Orient.

It would be getting far ahead of our story to note that Skeezix, under a distinctly less talented artist, remained remarkably young enough as well as foolish enough to enlist in the military for the Vietnam War. If he had gone to Madison from Tomah, he would more likely have joined the hugely popular antiwar movement. Some of the blame goes back to the original. King's own characters of the 1920s, like sympathetic versions of Sinclair Lewis's imaginary Minnesota village of the time, seem utterly unaware that a radical La Follette dynasty and its supportive farmer-labor reform movement are the most unique qualities of their own political landscape, the very thing that made Wisconsin, along with Minnesota and, to a lesser degree, the Dakotas, different and idealistic examples of the day rather than conformist and money-grubbing. Moreover, if the repair shop aspect of the strip happened to be set in Washington Park, Chicago, as King sometimes suggested, and where he continued to visit friends in a working garage, then we find something a bit worse for the rancorous 1920s. In a neighborhood lily white beginning to integrate, enraged whites of real life drove out would-be new black residents, for a time, with beatings and arson: in a phrase, it was Ku Klux Klan territory. Still more remarkably, Washington Park soon became a black neighborhood known for popular support of Communists and, much later, of Mayor Harold Washington and a certain senator named Obama. It was, in short, the opposite of King's white working-class paradise in which few black faces could be found (he treated a house maid and her boyfriend with sympathy, but drew them as in minstrelsy).

Would residents of Gasoline Alley, Wisconsin version, have been passive during the great events of the Depression and the New Deal era? Would they continue to support Republicans, Herbert Hoover in particular, during the depths of the Depression when Phil La Follette won the governorship twice over? Or were they perhaps an unacknowledged part of a regional farmers' holiday movement in the countryside—or simply participants in the Roosevelt landslide, a break from self-defeating individualism? Probably the *Chicago Tribune* management would not have accepted anything like these rebellious versions; *Little Orphan Annie*'s Daddy Warbucks spoke for management and the merchants of death (hence his name), and Patterson himself had long since abandoned the Midwest for Manhattan.

King's great visual adventures disappeared from the Sunday funnies by the middle 1930s, in any case, and his art had grown visibly tired by that time. It's understandable that the artist was happy to retire in the 1950s, leaving the work to other hands. Like viewers of an aging soap opera, veteran funny page readers had long since ceased to notice details, or at least it seems so. No matter, he had made his mark. The same rules would doubtless have applied to the less talented Smith, had he survived the 1935 automobile crash. Comics work was a good job that became a calling for King, probably never a calling for Smith, who saved his genius for private life.

In much the same spirit, Don Trachte (1915-2005) joined fellow Madisonian Carl Anderson (1865-1949) in the popular *Henry* strip. The Norwegian-American Anderson, a carpenter who found his way into comic strips and illustrations in the popular press, lost his place in the Depression and returned home in 1931. A chance encounter with a bald-headed boy used as a model in the art classes he taught led him to create the non-speaking Henry character, adopted by the *Saturday Evening Post*, who became a hit in the funny papers. Already in his sixties, Anderson needed help, and Trachte was close at hand, gradually assuming control of the Sunday color strip. A favorite, never published, remains mounted in the

Henry, created and drawn by Carl Anderson, and later by Don Trachte. Collection of George Hagenaur.

THE TOUGHEST YEAR OF HIS LIFE --
THAT SUMMER HE WORKED AT THE EDGEWATER!

Henry, relaxing at the Edgewater Hotel in Madison, Wisconsin. This one drawn by Don Trachte. Collection of the Edgewater Hotel.

21

Edgewater Hotel marking Trachte's memory of his summer as a young waiter there.

Henry, the bald kid with the chin dimple and no apparent capacity to speak, lives in an urban world of fairly mild terrors. An Old World–style (or German Wisconsin–style) butcher with cleaver in hand and a "Boy Wanted" sign beckons him, and he runs away: he clearly suspects that otherwise, he would be chopped up for chops. Sometimes Henry seems simple-minded, the joke shared among the funny page readers who may not be particularly bright or educated (from early on, wordless comics had a special appeal to immigrants who knew little English). Sometimes he seems more shrewd than his comic companions suspect. For a character who lasted so long, we never actually learn much about his life or character, not even why he is bald (ringworm would have been a familiar cause in the early decades of the strip). The acclaimed Ernie Bushmiller (*Nancy*), whose work was reprinted in Princeton, Wisconsin, during the 1980s, was considered by then to have created characters who mimicked "a moron on acid" (i.e., LSD), and this may be the Zen of Stupidity that Bill Griffith's *Zippy the Pinhead* exemplified in daily strips of the 1990s and later. But *Zippy* is deeply, profoundly ironic, a quality missing in *Henry*. In short: the enigma remains throughout Trachte's strip work. It is a Wisconsin enigma, as much as Anderson's sense of humor, but not Trachte's own enigma.

The exhaustion of early energy in the daily and Sunday funnies might hardly have been noticed if not for a burst of comic energy from other quarters. As comics genius (and *Mad* creator) Harvey Kurtzman was to put it, the comic *book* was the creation of "nameless, faceless laborers, toiling for a pittance in grungy studios, scorned by those in respectable trades and professions." If they had one advantage as artists and scriptwriters, it was that comic books were so ill-regarded that virtually no censorship or government control existed between the drawing board and the corner newsstand until the 1950s. The publishers and lead editors were not actually interested in art, of course; they were businessmen, some with extensive experience in the pulp magazine trades, who saw a profit to be made in

Zippy the Pinhead wakes up in Milwaukee. © 2000 by Bill Griffith.

a fairly wide-open field, and a host of talented youngsters (nearly all of them male) who were willing to work long hours for next to nothing. These studio sweatshops existed almost exclusively in Greater New York.

Tough Days for Wisconsin Comic Art

Thus our story of Wisconsin artists hits a notable low point. Chicago wasn't far from Milwaukee, Madison, or outlying areas, while New York was a long, long way to go away for a career. Besides, young people trained in art had other options, mainly commercial work of various kinds, drawing advertising material for wholesale and retail customers of some product line. Some of the best work for a handful of artists, including Gerald Gregg (1907–85), was close at hand. In Racine, Western Printing and Lithographing, a notable publisher for children and juveniles that began in 1907, peaked in its influence first with Big Little Books and then in partnership with Simon and Schuster published Golden Books until the firm's closure at the turn of the new century. Comics, actually small books with more comics than text, played a small part in Western's Big Little Books operation, and a handful of comics were published separately in the late 1930s and later on under contract with Disney. Illustrations, however, were crucial. Gregg joined the Western staff in 1935 and hit his career peak by 1943, as a noted innovator in cover illustrations for Dell paperbacks, also designed and published by Western. Today, he is seen by experts in the field as a master of the "noir" paperback cover.

A few other comic artists, closer to the usual lines of work and their art as well as their lives, are almost forgotten today. *Captain Midnight*, a radio serial show for kids that was a rousing success from 1938 to 1949, featured a comic book–style American hero who worked behind the scenes as an aviator on secret government missions. He stopped spies and other wrong-doers, but mainly Captain Midnight sold Ovaltine and premium items (for numbers of boxtops or labels), such as rings, telescopes, and the inevitable decoders (these last actually decrypted plot details from the next day's program!). Comics publishers, building upon such enthusiasms after Pearl

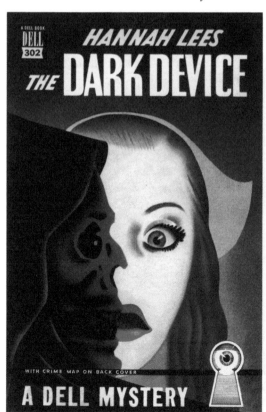

Cover art for Dell by Gerald Gregg.

23

Cover art for Dell by Gerald Gregg.

Harbor, put him into a comic book of his own in 1942–48—but transformed the Captain so thoroughly that he gained a superhero costume. A still less memorable newspaper strip version was drawn by Milwaukeean Erwin Hess, a commercial illustrator who spent three years with *Captain Midnight* dailies, 1942–45, with fellow Milwaukeean Henry Valleley, before moving on to a one-panel nostalgia

Captain Midnight, reproduction of original artwork by Erwin Hess. Collection of George Hagenaur.

feature, *The Good Old Days*, that continued until 1981 and may have reminded some readers of Clare Briggs's later work. On the side, Hess did a bit of art for *Gene Autry* comics. Yet another newspaper comics artist, Racine native Jack Crowe, transitioned his *Windy City Kitty*, a wartime strip that appeared in *Yank* and treated gender issues among the military in a kindly fashion, into a daily newspaper strip in Chicago and into civilian life. It did not survive long.

Comics and the daily newspapers continued to be surprisingly vital in the age of television, even in the afternoon dailies in their long, ultimately fatal downturn. It is often forgotten that publishers squeezed daily comics down to a size of their choice, during the Second World War, using paper shortages as rationale, and never returned to the size that artists themselves drew for. Comic books, it is likewise often forgotten, actually reached a postwar high in quality during the early 1950s. That they were also growing up when they were cut off by censorship and downright repression is a proper subject for the next chapter.

Windy City Kitty, reproduction of original artwork by Jack Crowe for *Yank.* Collection of George Hagenaur.

CHAPTER TWO
UNDERGROUND IN MADISON (AND MILWAUKEE)

Sometime in October 1968, comics artist Gilbert Shelton pulled up to my house on Spaight Street. You could see the old black Caddy coming a block away, and when he parked, the back window, full of stickers, tourist and hippie-LSD alike, offered an eyeful. Gilbert was a tall, tanned, well-built guy in his late twenties, a former University of Texas graduate student and sometime partygoer with Janis Joplin, but now on a mission, with a young, quiet blonde at his side. Already famous in Austin for *Feds 'N' Heads*, a dopey hippies-versus-cops strip appearing in the premier underground newspaper *The Rag*, he had some months earlier brought out a small comic under the same title with the same three heroes—Phineas, Freewheelin' Frank, and Fat Freddy. By this time, he was on his way to San Francisco, where would-be underground comix artists were in the process of gathering. He had come to Madison to collect $2,000, an enormous sum in the days when movies, dope, and beer were all cheap, rents mighty low, and genteel bohemian poverty, unbeknownst to ourselves, fast approaching its final days.

Feds 'N' Heads, © 1968 by Gilbert Shelton.

It had been my idea to put out a special issue of *Radical America*, the bimonthly journal that I published in the interests of Students for a Democratic Society (SDS), as a comic book. Robert Crumb's *Zap* #1 and *Zap* #0 (in that order, because the art had been mislaid for what would have been the first issue) had been published in San Francisco, and Gilbert wanted to create his own comics outfit, with a circle of pals mostly from Texas. The $2,000 actually came from an Old Left philanthropic entity, the Rabinowitz Foundation, and supplied a third of the amount needed to allow Rip Off Press to hit the ground running in January 1969, with *Radical America*

Komiks. George Mosse, the distinguished (and quietly gay) historian on the UW faculty, first thought he had been sent the wrong magazine for his subscription: I was supposed to be educating the young.

Radical America Komiks landed into one of the most fertile countercultures to be found anywhere on the planet in 1969, and those old enough will now

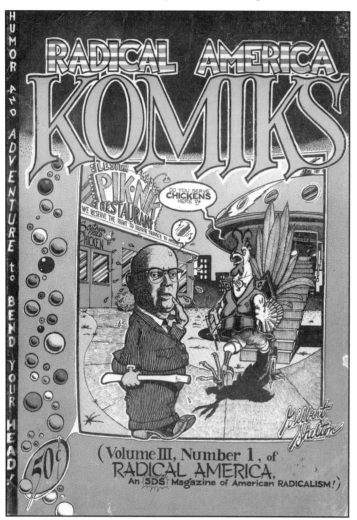

Radical America Komiks, © 1969 by Radical America, for SDS.

recall that the demographic/cultural maps of Madison seemed to have been redrawn wholesale within only a few years. Not that the vicinity of the campus and faculty zones of Madison's West Side had lacked a reputation for liberalism in the middle 1960s, and even a strong hint of old-time bohemianism here and there, young men and women "living together" without license, folk singers about, and marijuana for a smallish in-crowd. But these were mostly respectable—or at least kept behind closed doors. The explosion of rebellion on and around campus found an open gay and lesbianism shocking even to the closeted scene, garishly lovely outfits (with a rush on St. Vincent's resale store) for counterculturalists of all kinds, fairly open hallucinogen sales, and much, much more, confirming what rural legislators had always said about UW's corrupting influence. It doubtless compelled local police and FBI to pick and choose their targets: who to watch, who to pursue through a small army of semipro informers (budgets were high in those days), and who to phone-tap. The denizens of Bassett and Mifflin Streets in particular seemed to be living out a Freak Brothers strip of Shelton's, minus the cowboy outfits.

This scene calls for some serious historical backtracking. First to "bohemia," a concept dating to mid-nineteenth-century Paris, where young, arts-related and free-loving folks dug through resale shops to redesign themselves while setting an example that fascinated the middle classes across Europe and beyond. These

Excerpt from *Students for a Democratic Society, a Graphic History,* "The SDS Magazine," © 2008 by Paul Buhle and Gary Dumm.

NEXT DAY COMPOSING A LETTER TO GILBERT SHELTON, CREATOR OF WONDER WARTHOG...

GILBERT! I'VE BEEN SELLING "FEDS AND HEADS" AT THE SDS TABLE. AND A FOUNDATION JUST GAVE ME $2,000. ENOUGH FOR YOU TO DO THE COMIC!

AND SO, IN SAN FRANCISCO, GILBERT SHELTON BEGINS WORKING...

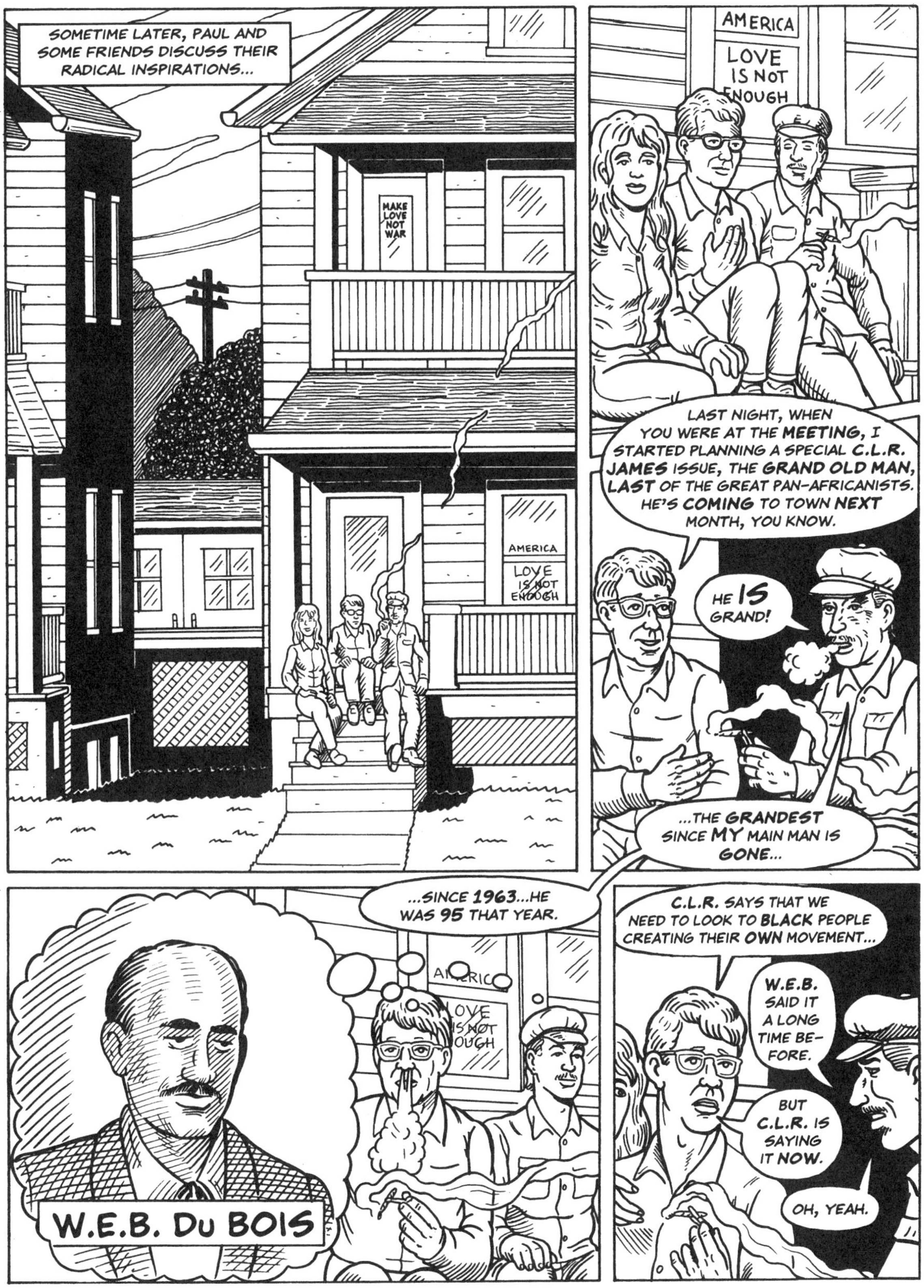
SOMETIME LATER, PAUL AND SOME FRIENDS DISCUSS THEIR RADICAL INSPIRATIONS...
MAKE LOVE NOT WAR
AMERICA
LOVE IS NOT ENOUGH
AMERICA
LOVE IS NOT ENOUGH
LAST NIGHT, WHEN YOU WERE AT THE MEETING, I STARTED PLANNING A SPECIAL C.L.R. JAMES ISSUE, THE GRAND OLD MAN, LAST OF THE GREAT PAN-AFRICANISTS. HE'S COMING TO TOWN NEXT MONTH, YOU KNOW.
HE IS GRAND!
...THE GRANDEST SINCE MY MAIN MAN IS GONE...
...SINCE 1963...HE WAS 95 THAT YEAR.
W.E.B. Du BOIS
C.L.R. SAYS THAT WE NEED TO LOOK TO BLACK PEOPLE CREATING THEIR OWN MOVEMENT...
W.E.B. SAID IT A LONG TIME BE-FORE.
BUT C.L.R. IS SAYING IT NOW.
OH, YEAH.

C.L.R.! WE ARE PUBLISHING AN ANTHOLOGY OF YOUR WRITINGS IN "RADICAL AMERICA." THE FIRST ANTHOLOGY ANYWHERE...FOR SDSERS AND OTHERS.

BUTTER? COFFEE?

ONLY MARMALADE. AND TEA.

SO BRITISH!

THAT WAS LIFE IN COLONIAL TRINIDAD. WE ALSO LEARNED SHAKESPEARE, YOU KNOW. AND CRICKET. THAT WAS MY LIFE, CRICKET. SUCH A DISAPPOINTMENT TO MY PARENTS, THEY WANTED ME TO BE A LAWYER OR A POLITICIAN.

YOU CHOSE SPORTS.

AND THAT'S HOW I DECIDED TO BECOME A REVOLUTIONARY. THE WHITES WERE NO BETTER THAN US. I LEARNED THAT ON THE CRICKET PITCH.

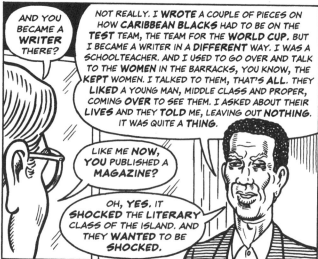

AND YOU BECAME A WRITER THERE?

NOT REALLY. I WROTE A COUPLE OF PIECES ON HOW CARIBBEAN BLACKS HAD TO BE ON THE TEST TEAM, THE TEAM FOR THE WORLD CUP. BUT I BECAME A WRITER IN A DIFFERENT WAY. I WAS A SCHOOLTEACHER. AND I USED TO GO OVER AND TALK TO THE WOMEN IN THE BARRACKS, YOU KNOW, THE KEPT WOMEN. I TALKED TO THEM, THAT'S ALL. THEY LIKED A YOUNG MAN, MIDDLE CLASS AND PROPER, COMING OVER TO SEE THEM. I ASKED ABOUT THEIR LIVES AND THEY TOLD ME, LEAVING OUT NOTHING. IT WAS QUITE A THING.

LIKE ME NOW, YOU PUBLISHED A MAGAZINE?

OH, YES. IT SHOCKED THE LITERARY CLASS OF THE ISLAND. AND THEY WANTED TO BE SHOCKED.

THEY STAYED AND YOU LEFT...

THEY WERE BROWN. I WAS BLACK.

...BUT YOU CAME BACK A REVOLUTIONARY.

A CAUTIOUS REVOLUTIONARY. THIS WAS IN 1959, BEFORE YOUR NEW LEFT. INDEPENDENCE WAS COMING. THE PRIME MINISTER HAD BEEN MY STUDENT, WHEN HE WAS STILL IN KNEE PANTS. HE CALLED ME BACK TO BE EDITOR OF THE PARTY PAPER. THEN THEY THREW ME OUT. BUT I STARTED OUR OWN NEW LEFT, WE CALLED IT NEW BEGINNINGS. IT WAS THE TRINIDADIAN SDS. AND WE HAD STOKELY CARMICHAEL UP HERE. HE IS A TRINIDADIAN, YOU KNOW.

AND NOW I'M PUBLISHING A MAGAZINE, FOR SDS. THE ISSUE OF YOUR WRITINGS WILL BE THE BIGGEST WE'VE EVER PUBLISHED. AND WILL REACH MORE PEOPLE.

MAKE SURE THEY GET IT IN ALL THE PLACES WHERE THEY KNOW ME...IN BRIXTON, THAT LONDON NEIGHBORHOOD, IN DETROIT, IN TORONTO AND MONTREAL AND JAMAICA AND IN ANTIGUA, TOO.

WE'LL GET THEM AROUND. ONE DOLLAR A COPY! SIXTY CENTS FOR FIVE OR MORE!

END

bohemians (so named for the opera *La Boheme*) were not so much revolutionary as personally libertarian, but indifferent to the accumulation of capital and the status seeking of the day's rising commercial class. The Greenwich Village bohemians of the 1910s, whose artists "discovered" the daily lives of ordinary people (and of sex workers, strippers to prostitutes), self-consciously built upon the foundation of those nineteenth-century Parisians and their modern-day counterparts. The young denizens of Madison's bohemian zones of the 1960s–70s and their successors definitely continued the traditions, right down to the look and feel of Williamson

Zippy visits Mondovi, Wisconsin. © 2007 by Bill Griffith.

("Willie") Street in the twenty-first century, with St. Vincent across the street from the alternative community's print shop with its defiant antiwar images in the window (for sale, inside).

But there was another, ambiguously connected tradition more pressing in the minds of the artists of *Radical America Komiks* and the comic art experiments to follow in Wisconsin: EC Comics and its successor, *Mad*, the most successful satire magazine in the twentieth century. There stands a story as big in its way as the rest of the American comics tradition combined.

Comic books, after the furious early development from clipped daily strips bound together and give-away advertising pamphlets, hit an all-time peak during the more prosperous and entertainment-starved Second World War. And then a sudden crisis, the first of many in the business cycles of comic books. Yesterday's superheroes had grown suddenly stale, and the readership, no longer including the huge captive audience of GIs overseas, was looking for something new without knowing what to look for. After some years of drift, a dash of sexualization (known as "Headlights" for the tight sweaters on women characters), and melodramatic crime comics, came something really startling: New Trend (1950-55).

These were the children of EC Comics, and like another EC offspring were to be the shaping influence upon the artistic conceptualizations of the underground generation. Some of them were horror comics, some were liberal-to-radical "message" comics about the grim side of the McCarthy era, some were science fiction comics suggesting the catastrophes ahead in the atomic age—war, genetic mutation, and so on. One of New Trend's most remarkable was a series devoted to an exact history of wars over the ages by the brilliant young artist-editor Harvey Kurtzman, whose 1972 appearance in Milwaukee caused so much of a stir.

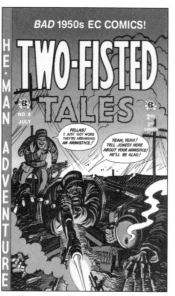

Kurtzman's *Two-Fisted Tales,* 1951.

These New Trend comics were, first of all, the most thoroughly researched historical comics that had ever appeared on American newsstands. The stories ranged back to Roman times and earlier, coming forward through the tales of European conquerors at home and in the New World, partaking, of course, of the American Revolution and the Civil War but also Indian wars, the U.S. invasion of Cuba in the Spanish-American War, First and Second World Wars—and Korea. Only perhaps realist war novels by the likes of James Jones and Norman Mailer and a small handful of daring films, such as *A Walk in the Sun,* could compare as popular, realistic entertainment. Not all the details, moreover, came from library research books. Kurtzman and his friends had themselves gone through the recent antifascist war, and servicemen who read EC Comics eagerly supplied information that, the editors claimed, could not have been found elsewhere.

Occasionally, Kurtzman and his artists even told them from the viewpoint of enemy combatants and civilians. War, it turned out, was the real enemy, the look of dead and wounded soldiers as dreadful as anything in *The Vault of Horror.*

EC publisher William Gaines was looking for more work to pile on Kurtzman, who admired the fearless college humor magazines flourishing among the ex-GIs. *Mad Comics* (1952-55) started slowly, but Gaines covered early losses, and soon gained a fanatically loyal readership. Readers proudly enrolled themselves in the half-satirical "Fan Addicts," a true subversive (and largely Jewish) organization of its day and age.

EC soon paid the price. An early issue of *Panic,* an in-house knockoff of *Mad,* was seized in Boston for ridiculing Santa Claus, while another issue was grabbed by the New York police (who also arrested one of Gaines's assistants). In 1954, Gaines may have made a mistake in volunteering to testify at congressional hearings without a cadre of fellow publishers; he believed that he could reason away the anxieties with sentiments that must have sounded like another form of treason to the cold war politicians of the day. American children were by and large healthy of mind; it was the would-be censors who saw filth and perversion. Delinquency, consequently, was a

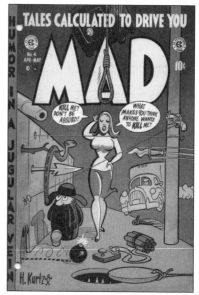

Harvey Kurtzman's *Mad.*

social problem not to be whisked away with uncensored comics. "Our problems are economic and social and they are complex. Our people need understanding; they need to have affection, decent homes, decent food," he said. It was pure New Dealism.

They were having none of it. The new Comics Code, written in part by the creators of Archie Comics, commanded servility. (EC had its revenge in small ways, such as a devastating satire, "Starchie," in a 1955 issue of *Mad*, with Archie and Jughead as the real juvenile delinquents.) Days before  the Comics Code took effect, Gaines suspended his horror and suspense comics and placed his trust in Kurtzman's vision. What the artist-writer wanted was something strikingly new, so new that there were no real models for it. After a series of daunting developments, including Kurtzman's demand to have a controlling interest in the new magazine, the smoke cleared. Horror veteran Al Feldstein would be editor. Kurtzman and most of the artists, including his confidant and key collaborator, Will Elder, went along with their boss. *Mad* magazine lost the edginess of *Mad Comics*, although it remained (and still remains, much reduced in circulation and influence) on the side of liberalism.

From the first issue three years earlier, *Mad* had a Kurtzman-esque flavor, an almost indefinable (but definitely Jewish) take on popular culture as fascinating but also prone to corruption, including the endless cliché. *Mad* only continued to get madder for the next three years and twenty-five issues. The apex, by critical acclaim, was "What's My Shine," an attack on the Red-baiting in the Army-McCarthy hearings that brought the drama home to so many citizens of McCarthy's own state. Shortly before transformation into magazine format free from comic book industry censorship, *Mad* announced in its October 1954 issue that it was headed "underground," a word that during the middle 1950s still recalled wartime partisans fighting behind fascist lines. In one panel, a subversive-looking comics publisher is peddling comics on a street corner to a child, and in the next, the pseudo-documentation of a "comic book raid," we see a criminal-appearing cartoonist, and another with three eyes (i.e., an alien), "rounded up in their hideout," all contemporary dangers rolled up into one.

Indeed. Alongside the congressional hearings and century's biggest Red scare was the less-remembered comic book scare, which led to actual book burnings. Reported intermittently in the middle 1950s (and likely occurring more frequently than researchers have yet discovered), these events seem to have been organized around Catholic lay institutions and aimed at the presumed threat of juvenile delinquency "caused" by children reading comics, but also at the sexuality, social criticism, and anything that might be made to seem "foreign" (in the rural Midwest, often perceived as created in New York by people with Jewish-sounding names).

In the small community of Stone Bank, midway between Madison and

Milwaukee, housewife Ruth Lutwitzi launched her own campaign by gathering comic books and marking them up for any signs of sexuality in particular. Active in the American Legion Auxiliary's Child Welfare Department, Lutwitzi gave lectures to PTAs, organized a mass trade-in of comics from kids, and personally set 546 comics aflame in a yard outside the Stone Bank grade school. Child donors were given a "good" book (hardbound) and a letter congratulating them on their Americanism. A local grade-school teacher commented decades later that the book burning seemed terribly wrong and the children had been pressured to take part; but he had wanted to keep his job, and kept quiet.

The unsuccessful, Madison-based battle of the "Joe Must Go" committees to deny Joseph McCarthy reelection a few years earlier does not seem to have raised any comic book issues, and the liberal parents in the countercrusade may possibly have disapproved of comics for their own children. Still, Frank Zeidler remained the Socialist mayor of Milwaukee until 1960, no small thing or personal anomaly, even if Zeidler's personal popularity far exceeded socialistic public sympathies. In a sense, the die had already been cast for the 1960s on cultural as well as political grounds. Radicals of some type had been facing off against conservatives for generations in Wisconsin, often over issues of public education and sometimes on issues of the right to dissent. A Wisconsin legislator, Reuben C. Peterson, argued in the middle 1950s so resolutely against a bill to ban the sale of "dangerous" comics to children ("I tried to tell them that we have such a thing as a First Amendment," he recalled decades later) that he was booed from the

Back cover of *Zap Comix #0,* by R. Crumb. Published by Apex Novelty, 1967.

statehouse floor. In the end, the repressive legislation did not pass. The fever seemed to ease nationally, although conservatives never permanently abandoned the issue and Senator Joseph Lieberman of Connecticut, the hawkish Democratic vice-presidential candidate for 2000, could still be heard in the twenty-first century urging legal suppression of undesirable lyrics, films, and television. By that time, comics had long since become less important, and committees of comics scholars and publishers had been working hard for decades with great success to fend off censorship.

Back in 1969, no one would have predicted that underground comix would make a start in Wisconsin, along with San Francisco and Berkeley, or that alternative comics of the most remarkable and daring kinds would blossom in midstate Princeton, north of Madison, within a decade. Or for that matter, that several of the stars of twenty-first-century art comics were to trace their origins back to these parts. Seen differently, however, it was all very Madisonian, even Milwaukeean.

The *x* factor that changed comics to comix was first seen in San Francisco, in the poster shops where Day-Glo images and photos of very angry-looking Black Panthers pioneered a poster print business with advertising big enough to keep *Ramparts* magazine, then master of muckraking journalism, going for years. Young Robert Crumb was the foremost artist, by a long shot, but along with him came a dozen highly talented, definitely leftwing comics veterans, the oldest of them still not thirty, a pack of them (including Art Spiegelman) from New York. There were a handful of comix in traditional comic book form, but they had twenty-four to forty-eight pages, black-and-white insides, and a pricetag of fifty cents or a dollar. That was not, however, the way comix first reached tens of thousands of readers.

Comix could first be found nationwide in the underground press, whose Madison version, *Connections*, was one of the best anywhere. *Connections* reprinted comix from San Francisco but also launched a local artist, Nick Thorkelson, grandson of a UW administrator decades earlier and brother of Monkee Peter Tork. Thorkelson was practically the staff artist ("practically" because no one was paid at *Connections* and no one quite figured out the contents, one issue to the next). He had been reading *Mad Comics* and *Mad Magazine* since childhood, and he fashioned a takeoff on an extremely well-circulated and LSD-laced strip by Gilbert Shelton, "Set My Chickens Free." Thorkelson retitled it "The Day I Set My Gangsters on My Freaks" and redirected the narrative metaphorically, unforgettably, at the cops swinging clubs at freaky-looking undergrads in the Dow riot on the UW campus in October 1967. It wasn't brilliant comic art but it contained memorable strokes. It made Madison comix (and comics) history.

The Madison/comix connection with Shelton doubled through the appearance of *Radical America Komiks* fifteen months later. This one-shot comic sold best at the Electric Eye, a head shop that boasted bongs, posters, and hippie jewelry by local artisans. It was certainly the first comic book of any kind produced *for* Madison, unless there had been promotional comic books here that various companies created elsewhere for customers during the 1940s–50s. Despite its 30,000 print run, copies of *RA Komiks* seem to have disappeared, but you can see it today on the Web, within the virtual files of *Radical America*. Who knew that a hyperphase for

"The Day I Set My Gangsters on My Freaks," by Nick Thorkelson for Madison's *Connections*, 1967.

Excerpt from "Smiling Sergeant Death and his Merciless Mayhem Patrol," page 2, by Gilbert Shelton. From *Radical America Komiks*, 1969.

Excerpt from "Smiling Sergeant Death and His Merciless Mayhem Patrol," page 9, featuring Gilbert Shelton's Wonder Wart-Hog. From *Radical America Komiks,* 1969.

Excerpt from "The Freaks Pull a Heist!" featuring Gilbert Shelton's Fabulous Furry Freak Brothers. From *Radical America Komiks*, 1969.

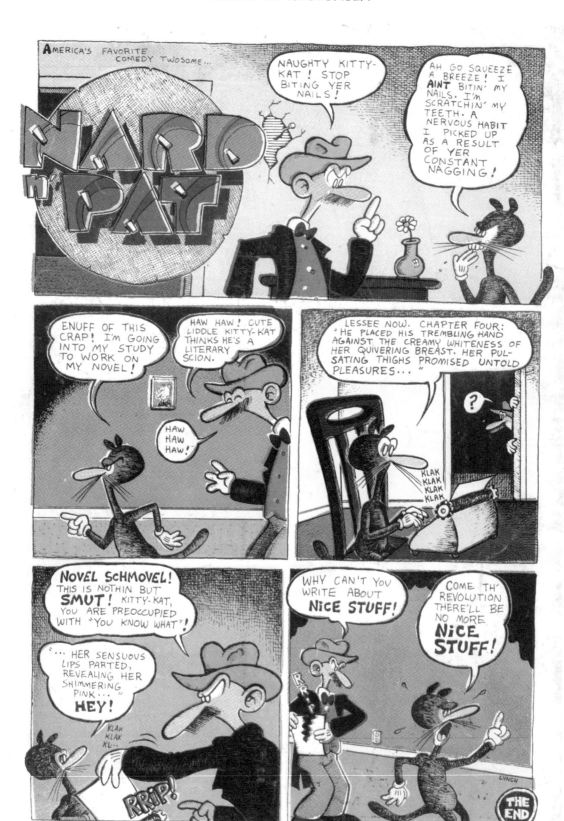

Nard n' Pat by Jay Lynch as it appeared on the back cover of *Radical America Komiks*, 1969.

Wisconsin, after the modest *RA Komiks*, lay just ahead?

Actually, there was already a glimmer in Milwaukee, whose hipsters (and there were quite a few) considered Madison, just up the road, to be a youth culture nirvana. Denis Kitchen, a near-local lad (graduate of a Racine high school) and boy socialist (he ran for lieutenant governor on the Socialist Labor Party ticket in 1970), was thinking hard about producing his own comics. He made himself art director of a somewhat political hippie weekly, the *Madison-Milwaukee Bugle American*, launched the same year of his candidacy, with a near-full page of comics. The comics page marked a first for Madison's alternative press. The artists were

Denis Kitchen's cover for the *Madison Bugle-American* #1, 1979.

strictly local talent: Milwaukeeans Don Glassford, Jim Mitchell, Bruce Walters, and Wendell Pugh, plus Kitchen himself who, when he wasn't organizing talent, had a fine wit and a devilish impulse to poke fun at radicals as well as conservatives.

Ad for the *Madison Bugle-American*, 1979.

By 1970, *Connections* had died and some Madisonians were bereft of a radical news and commentary outlet. *Madison Kaleidoscope,* a quasi-successor, had a future comics-and-film scholar, Dave Wagner, at the helm. It ran few comics, and after Wagner quit, some staff members broke with *Kaleidoscope* to publish *King Street Trolley* and later, *Takeover!,* one of the more hyperventilating revolutionary tabloids of the day. There were also pressing political reasons for this series of reorientations: the bombing of the Army Math Research Center on the UW campus in August 1970 brought a wave of anxiety among peaceniks at large (the blast killed a researcher in the building) and a sense that an era had passed. Madison was to become a progressive, countercultural capital, ironically part of its status as the state's capital because state workers would become a reliable bloc of sympathetic voters. The revolution was, however, not happening, or at least not as the revolutionaries had imagined.

Yet another fresh tabloid for 1970, the *Madison Bugle-American*, one might say, met the appearance of a new era with a more hippie-cultural live-and-let-live approach than the hardened radicals of *Takeover*. While the *Bugle* soon became a Milwaukee-based paper with statewide circulation and some Madison features, the hardliners found a comics genius by accident. Ironically, it was in the planning

Sharon Rudahl's *A Dangerous Woman*, published by The New Press, 2007.

stage of *Takeover* that the prospective editors convinced a young artist in town, Sharon Rudahl, to be the paper's art editor. Soon to become one of the best known of the women's underground comix artists and later author-artist of the graphic biography of Emma Goldman, *A Dangerous Woman*, Rudahl was mainly an illustrator in her Madison days but a keen-eyed one. Her somewhat but not

Two-page excerpt from *A Dangerous Woman*, ©2007 by Sharon Rudahl.

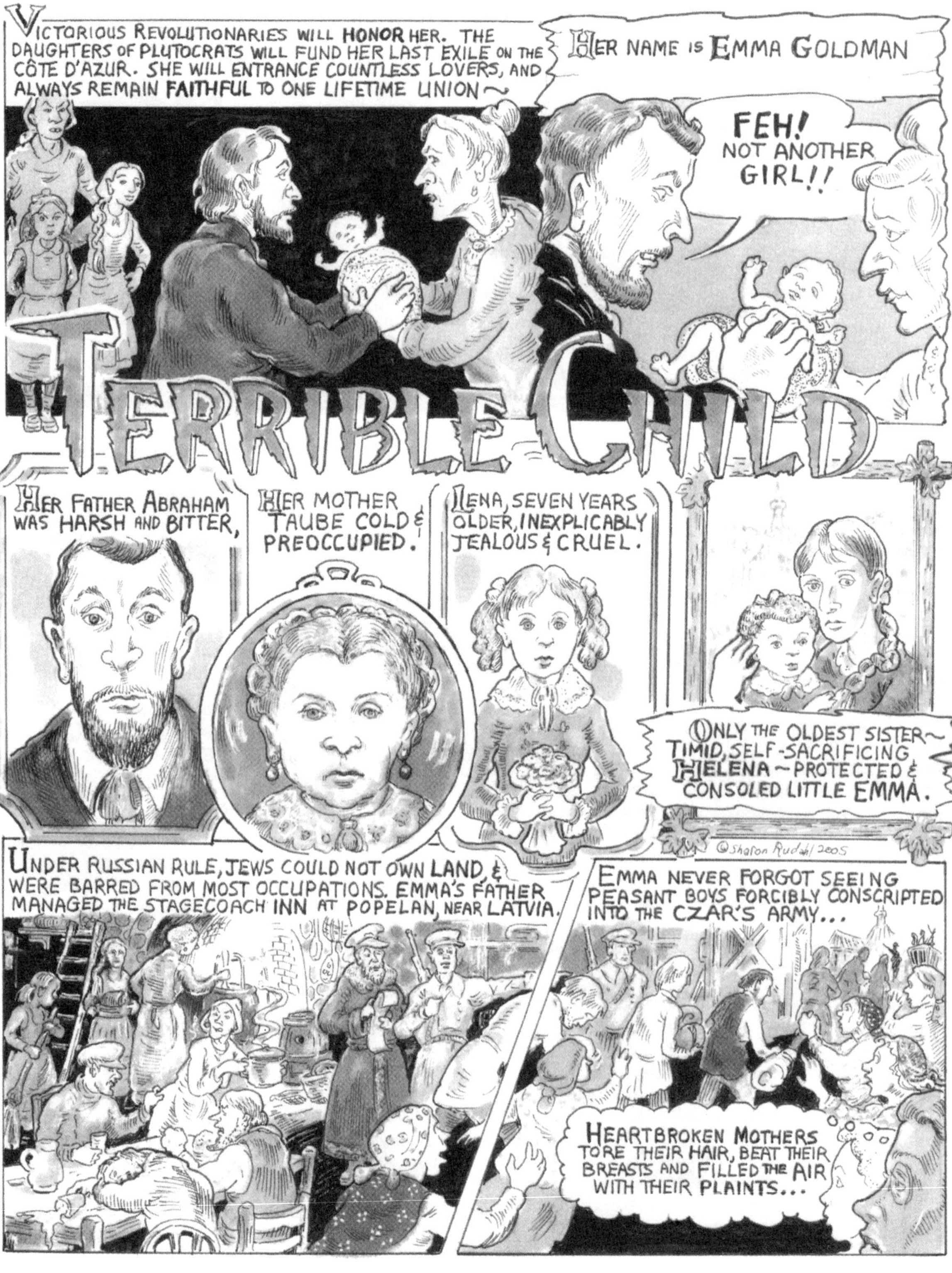

VICTORIOUS REVOLUTIONARIES WILL HONOR HER. THE DAUGHTERS OF PLUTOCRATS WILL FUND HER LAST EXILE ON THE CÔTE D'AZUR. SHE WILL ENTRANCE COUNTLESS LOVERS, AND ALWAYS REMAIN FAITHFUL TO ONE LIFETIME UNION~
HER NAME IS EMMA GOLDMAN
FEH! NOT ANOTHER GIRL!!
TERRIBLE CHILD
HER FATHER ABRAHAM WAS HARSH AND BITTER,
HER MOTHER TAUBE COLD & PREOCCUPIED.
LENA, SEVEN YEARS OLDER, INEXPLICABLY JEALOUS & CRUEL.
ONLY THE OLDEST SISTER~ TIMID, SELF-SACRIFICING HELENA~PROTECTED & CONSOLED LITTLE EMMA.
©Sharon Rudahl 2005
UNDER RUSSIAN RULE, JEWS COULD NOT OWN LAND, & WERE BARRED FROM MOST OCCUPATIONS. EMMA'S FATHER MANAGED THE STAGECOACH INN AT POPELAN, NEAR LATVIA.
EMMA NEVER FORGOT SEEING PEASANT BOYS FORCIBLY CONSCRIPTED INTO THE CZAR'S ARMY...
HEARTBROKEN MOTHERS TORE THEIR HAIR, BEAT THEIR BREASTS AND FILLED THE AIR WITH THEIR PLAINTS...

entirely satirical look backward from the middle 1970s, an anthology comic of 1976 published by Kitchen Sink, is the hands-down memorable strip treating Madison's avowed revolutionary political counterculture.

By the early 1970s, new comix were flowing out of the Bay Area by the dozens and then hundreds per year, with hardly anything from historic pulp publishing center New York, or anywhere else, including Chicago, where a start had trickled off into near-nothing. Kitchen and his friends, however, could be seen back in 1969 hawking issues of his first book production, *Mom's Homemade Comics #1*, at Milwaukee's own Schlitz Circus Parade, until halted by cops alerted to Kitchen's cheerful drawings of ladies' breasts. Taking over the production of *Bijou*, a Chicago-based anthology famed for its drawings by Skip Williamson and Jay Lynch, Kitchen Sink found commercial success. After a few more early comics, Crumb's *Home Grown Funnies* began selling like hot cakes, eventually reaching 160,000 copies. In Wisconsin as well as the Bay Area, a new era of comic book production was thus underway, with furtive connections to past comic eras. Kitchen personally did the footwork, flyers, radio, and television for Harvey Kurtzman's visit to the Free University at UW-Milwaukee. The enthusiastic crowd

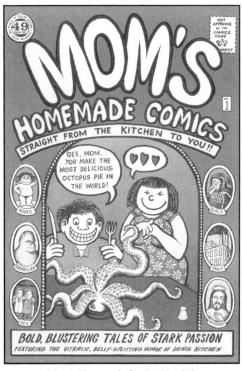

Mom's Homemade Comics #1, 1969.

proved that comics history was alive in Wisconsin, endeared the comics giant to Kitchen, and laid some groundwork for what would become the most significant of Kitchen Sink's archives projects.

Zippy visits the world's largest muskie in Hayward, Wisconsin. © 2002 by Bill Griffith.

Excerpt from R. Crumb's "Whiteman Meets Bigfoot." From *Home Grown Funnies,* Kitchen Sink's first bestseller.

"Wisconsin Story," by Sharon Rudahl, published in *Snarf* #6, 1975. Cover art by R. Crumb.

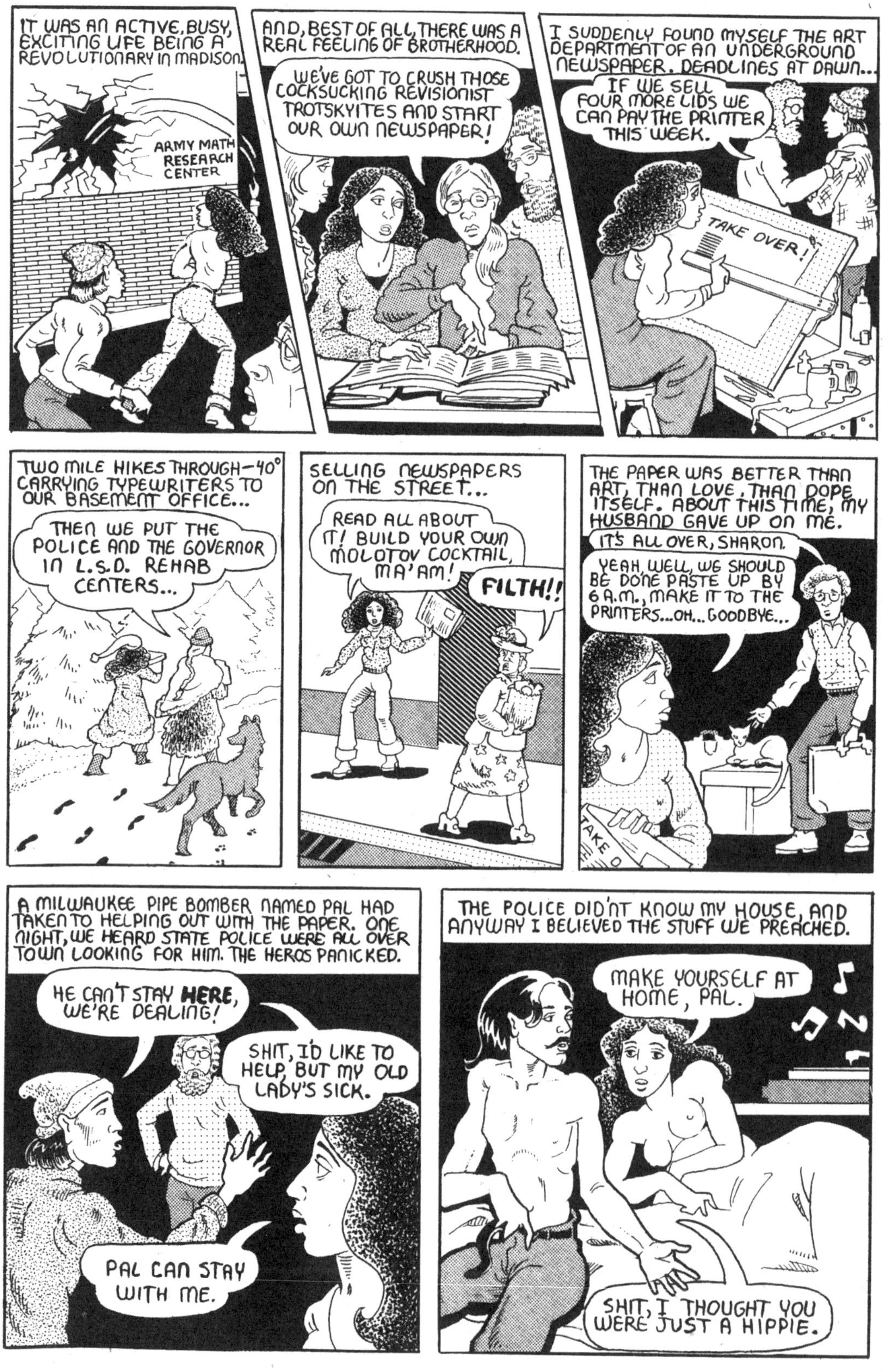
IT WAS AN ACTIVE, BUSY, EXCITING LIFE BEING A REVOLUTIONARY IN MADISON.
ARMY MATH RESEARCH CENTER
AND, BEST OF ALL, THERE WAS A REAL FEELING OF BROTHERHOOD.
WE'VE GOT TO CRUSH THOSE COCKSUCKING REVISIONIST TROTSKYITES AND START OUR OWN NEWSPAPER!
I SUDDENLY FOUND MYSELF THE ART DEPARTMENT OF AN UNDERGROUND NEWSPAPER. DEADLINES AT DAWN...
IF WE SELL FOUR MORE LIDS WE CAN PAY THE PRINTER THIS WEEK.
TAKE OVER!
TWO MILE HIKES THROUGH -40° CARRYING TYPEWRITERS TO OUR BASEMENT OFFICE...
THEN WE PUT THE POLICE AND THE GOVERNOR IN L.S.D. REHAB CENTERS...
SELLING NEWSPAPERS ON THE STREET...
READ ALL ABOUT IT! BUILD YOUR OWN MOLOTOV COCKTAIL, MA'AM!
FILTH!!
THE PAPER WAS BETTER THAN ART, THAN LOVE, THAN DOPE ITSELF. ABOUT THIS TIME, MY HUSBAND GAVE UP ON ME.
IT'S ALL OVER, SHARON.
YEAH, WELL, WE SHOULD BE DONE PASTE UP BY 6 A.M., MAKE IT TO THE PRINTERS...OH... GOODBYE...
A MILWAUKEE PIPE BOMBER NAMED PAL HAD TAKEN TO HELPING OUT WITH THE PAPER. ONE NIGHT, WE HEARD STATE POLICE WERE ALL OVER TOWN LOOKING FOR HIM. THE HEROS PANICKED.
HE CAN'T STAY HERE, WE'RE DEALING!
SHIT, I'D LIKE TO HELP, BUT MY OLD LADY'S SICK.
PAL CAN STAY WITH ME.
THE POLICE DIDN'T KNOW MY HOUSE, AND ANYWAY I BELIEVED THE STUFF WE PREACHED.
MAKE YOURSELF AT HOME, PAL.
SHIT, I THOUGHT YOU WERE JUST A HIPPIE.

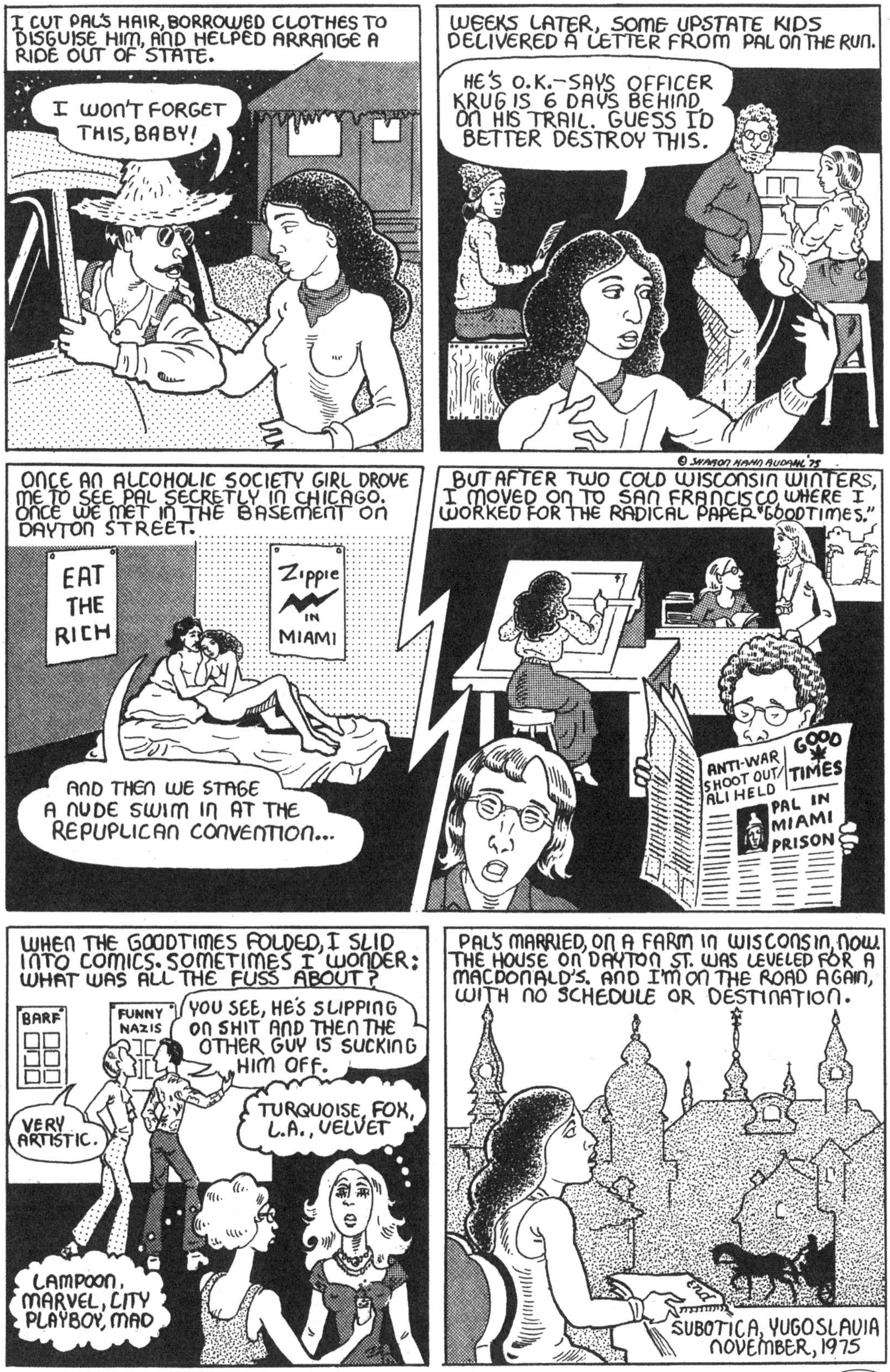
I CUT PAL'S HAIR, BORROWED CLOTHES TO DISGUISE HIM, AND HELPED ARRANGE A RIDE OUT OF STATE.
I WON'T FORGET THIS, BABY!
WEEKS LATER, SOME UPSTATE KIDS DELIVERED A LETTER FROM PAL ON THE RUN.
HE'S O.K.–SAYS OFFICER KRUG IS 6 DAYS BEHIND ON HIS TRAIL. GUESS I'D BETTER DESTROY THIS.
© SHARON KAHN RUDAHL '75
ONCE AN ALCOHOLIC SOCIETY GIRL DROVE ME TO SEE PAL SECRETLY IN CHICAGO. ONCE WE MET IN THE BASEMENT ON DAYTON STREET.
EAT THE RICH
Zippie IN MIAMI
AND THEN WE STAGE A NUDE SWIM IN AT THE REPUPLICAN CONVENTION...
BUT AFTER TWO COLD WISCONSIN WINTERS, I MOVED ON TO SAN FRANCISCO WHERE I WORKED FOR THE RADICAL PAPER "GOODTIMES."
ANTI-WAR SHOOT OUT/ ALI HELD
GOOD TIMES
PAL IN MIAMI PRISON
WHEN THE GOODTIMES FOLDED, I SLID INTO COMICS. SOMETIMES I WONDER: WHAT WAS ALL THE FUSS ABOUT?
BARF
FUNNY NAZIS
YOU SEE, HE'S SLIPPING ON SHIT AND THEN THE OTHER GUY IS SUCKING HIM OFF.
VERY ARTISTIC.
TURQUOISE, FOX, L.A., VELVET
LAMPOON, MARVEL, CITY PLAYBOY, MAD
PAL'S MARRIED, ON A FARM IN WISCONSIN, NOW. THE HOUSE ON DAYTON ST. WAS LEVELED FOR A MACDONALD'S. AND I'M ON THE ROAD AGAIN, WITH NO SCHEDULE OR DESTINATION.
End
SUBOTICA, YUGOSLAVIA NOVEMBER, 1975

END

Back in late 1971 Denis Kitchen and Jim Mitchell traveled to California to meet up with as many of the resident comix artists as possible. They began a "jam," a cartoon to which numerous artists contribute. The panels above are a section from that jam. Robert Crumb has also contributed. This strip was never completed.

Zippy visits the world's largest billiard balls in Madison, Wisconsin. © 2005 by Bill Griffith.

CHAPTER THREE
HOW COMICS BECOME HISTORY AND EVEN ART

Around 1970–72, American popular culture and culture at large seemed to turn upon its axis. "Oldies" music stations blossomed, giving a lot of aural space to Don McLean's "Bye, Bye, Miss American Pie" and FM stations featured Bruce Springsteen's various recollections of something lost in culture, something evidently beyond regaining. The past became a bigger subject, within marketable popular culture, than it had been since at least the 1930s (the recession didn't hurt this trend: the seventies felt a little like the Depression, at least for the millions of jobless). But if the Depression images recalled mostly rural or small town life, the new nostalgia was for the created world of modern culture, albeit in an earlier version. No one got it earlier or better, in the underground comix setting, than Robert Crumb with his loving depiction of retro signage, street feeling in metropolis or small town, of the 1920s–40s, the way things looked more interesting to his eyes than the bland reality of the suburbanized present.

Scholars also came along, an important development in itself, lending legitimacy to a way of seeing the world through the unprecedented scale of campus graduate students and undergrads. The *Journal of Popular Culture* milieu created its academic niche mainly through conventions of the Popular Culture Association, featuring along with professors and graduate students various television writers and executives and comic artists of past or present, forging and dignifying a fandom previously restricted to groupies and collectors. For that matter, the increase in the number of collectors was no small part of the picture for comic art, because "originals" previously tossed out now possessed value of some kind. That is to say, comics began to resemble the art market. It would be a couple more decades before the scholarship made its way into the mainstream of academia, but topics previously off limits, including comics, now sneaked in with the generation that had shortly before intimidated professors by striking and setting up picket lines around buildings. As a Parisian student quipped: after 1968, any topic was likely to be acceptable . . . even comics.

Arguments could be made for the world of art proper that Warhol and Lichtenstein blew apart the fixed triumph of abstract expressionism and that pop art was the real avant-garde of the 1960s. A better argument here would probably include the rise of Larry Rivers, whose political joking about the founding fathers, likewise his open bisexuality and his incorporation of popular cultural scraps into visual constructions, added up to a virtual pop revival of Dada. Like the avalanche of respected women's art soon to follow, Rivers's work helped set the mood for something far beyond Clement Greenberg and the aging cold war avant-garde, so-called, of the *Partisan Review* and the CIA-sponsored Congress for Cultural Freedom. The next step highlighted refiguration, the recognizable human figure, and hinted where it did not spell out the return of a coherent narrative, something treated by *Partisan Review,* and related "New York intellectual" circles, as akin to socialist realism and its supposed partner, Red totalitarianism. The ensconced critics still held the high ground of the prestigious intelligentsia, but it was fast giving way after the box-office triumph of x-rated *Midnight Cowboy* (scripted by a victim of the Hollywood Blacklist and condemned by the cold war crowd as bad for America), the defeats of the U.S. in Vietnam, and the rise of comix and the counterculture.

Cultural Correspondence (1975–83), self-described as the first journal published for intellectuals unashamed of watching television, took life with current and former Madisonians, including a returnee or two. For most of its limited life, its editors met in Madison and managed to produce an issue or so per year. Comics were a constant in these pages, not originals but interviews with artists and discussion of what underground comix meant, now that the peak had come and gone. The magazine ended up in my hands when Dave Wagner became embroiled in the Madison newspaper strike and the publication of a strikers' daily paper. But among its other editors were the leading American Studies scholar of popular culture, George Lipsitz, and another important cultural historian, Daniel Czitrom (whose *Media and the American Mind* soon was to become a classic of the field). It was a successor journal to *Radical America,* even while the latter continued to exist until 1993, itself covering comics history occasionally and publishing drawings by Nick Thorkelson (for a while, in Somerville, Massachusetts, he was on the editorial board along with several other Madison refugees). Eventually, in the 1980s, a special issue of *RA* appeared as *An Underhanded History of America,* the most ambitious comics history until *A People's History of American Empire* twenty years later. Thorkelson did the drawing, while Jim O'Brien, a former Madison SDS stalwart, graduate student, and *RA* editor, provided the script.

And yet, for all this enthusiasm, the development of comics in Wisconsin owed itself mainly to someone outside this circle: Denis Kitchen. A 1968 UW-Milwaukee graduate who had lived at home until his junior year, he was drafted but so lanky in his six-four frame that he tested too thin after three weeks and was discharged. He had been art editor and sole cartoonist of *Snide,* a one-shot UW-M humor magazine, and thus prepared to jump into some larger operation. He was also a dedicated socialist of the old-fashioned, working-class variety who would devote his first comic materials to his windmill-tilting campaign for lieutenant governor, using the campaign to renew the old class-versus-class themes that Wisconsinites once knew so well (agree or disagree).

How all this lines up with his subsequent world of comic production offers a fascinating subject with no certain answers—even from Kitchen himself. Perhaps the world of past comics recalled a Wisconsin that looked different before the industries began to close and the bankers, in and out of state, seized more and more control of the political life that the La Follettes had strived to retain for the people's business. Or was it a source of fascination for a young comic artist drawn to the traditions of the trade, an opportunity to make a business work in interesting ways with interesting people?

In any case, when Kitchen established Kitchen Sink publications in Princeton, Wisconsin, its influence loomed huge in one key respect: It revived the memory of a handful of giants of the comics field, including Al Capp, Milton Caniff, Harvey Kurtzman, Will Eisner, Ernie Bushmiller (if *Nancy* is indeed a classic and its artist a giant), among other lesser talents, in ways that stood

Krazy Kat

apart from the nostalgia-bent republication of *Little Nemo* and *Krazy Kat* among a very few other comic icons with work reprinted in book form during the 1960s and 1970s. Kitchen Sink's output in the format of comics rapidly became a foundation for future comic art, a living history embedded in a wider field of comic art history than had previously been accepted by anyone except small numbers of fannish enthusiasts.

This was not Kitchen Sink's only role, by a long shot. If it had published nothing more than *Gay Comix*, launched in 1976 with Howard Cruse as editor, and *Wet Satin*, women's erotic comics

ERNIE BUSHMILLER'S NANCY

Nancy Eats Food

INTRODUCTION BY BILL GRIFFITH

Ernie Bushmiller's *Nancy Eats Food*, 1989.

edited by Trina Robbins, it would have achieved a certain niche in comics history. But Kitchen Sink also published multitudinous anthologies and no less than a half-dozen series, brought scores of fresh comic artists to print, kept the pioneers of the 1960s underground comix field going, and even seemed, for a moment, to bridge the gap to the comic book mainstream. Thanks

Gay Comix #1, 1980. Cover by Rand Holmes.

55

Excerpt from "The Crush," © 1986 by Alison Bechdel in *Gay Comix* #10. Cover art by Peter Keane.

Top: Robert Crumb drew this letterhead for Kitchen Sink Press in 1985.

Left: Cover of *Comix Book* #1, by Peter Poplaski, 1974. (See p. 60)

Right: Cover of *Blab!* #3, by Charles Burns, 1988.

57

Excerpt from "Piano Lessons Paid Off for Liberace," by Bill Griffith in *Sleazy Scandals of the Silver Screen*, published by Kitchen Sink, 1978. Cover by Art Spiegelman.

Consumer Comix, published by Kitchen Sink and the Wisconsin Department of Consumer Affairs, 1975. (See p. 65) Cover art by Denis Kitchen, Peter Loft, and Pete Poplaski.

to an arrangement with mainstream comics giant Stan Lee, *Comix Book* appeared in the middle 1970s, three issues, good payment (by the day's standards), and a newsstand presence nationally. Unfortunately, like so many other efforts to bring alternative comics to a wider audience, this particular one did not succeed. Still, the scope of Kitchen Sink's output and the growing sense that comics had a history and a continuous development beyond the early-fading underground scene proved to be of inestimable importance.

The crisis that fell upon the undergrounds, eclipsing the most talented generation of artists since the 1940s and early 1950s, had its origins in the decline of the counterculture at large after the early 1970s. The belief that American society could become radically different and more egalitarian died as hard as it had after the New Deal, and the triumph of a warrior Right was just as demoralizing. Indeed, the government investigations and cultural shutdown of the 1950s were mirrored in the Intelpro actions against political groups and the underground press, busts of head shops that sold underground comix essentially part of the operation.

This time around, real Reds were few (the Black Panthers and Native American activists were the real victims of massive and violent repression). The women's and gay movements were literally on the march, and if culture generally carried the banner when politics collapsed into conservative or imperial consensus, by the 1970s–80s it did so even more. English department scholars and grad students invented new languages to explain the impossibility of change under Ronald Reagan and the necessity to wrestle with Freud and Foucault rather than Marx. Soon enough, those languages would themselves languish. For the moment, and for those intellectuals grappling with a need or at least a desire for intelligent entertainment, comics were coming of age.

The struggle for a small-scale comics empire in a former mukluks factory is another side of the Wisconsin comics story. Thanks to a strategic error (a board game called Libido that bombed), the business (called Krupp, in a joking Wisconsin-German way) behind the comics nearly collapsed in late 1972. Kitchen, his wife, and child moved to a Princeton farm, and a second child was born a few months later. He rented an office and warehouse in town and relocated the operation by stages.

Zippy, © 2003 by Bill Griffith.

Top: A Kitchen Sink fifteen-year anniversary party invite drawn by Kitchen, Pete Poplaski, and Donald Simpson, 1985.

Bottom left: Krupp Comic Works ad from 1970.

Bottom right: Poster from 1976 promoting *Cartoon-O-Rama!*, a variety show which included appearances of R. Crumb's band, the Cheap Suit Serenaders, Harvey Kurtzman, editorial cartoonist Bill Sanders (from Oshkosh, Wis.), and *Brenda Starr* creator Dale Messick.

THE **BIRTH** OF **COMIX BOOK**

I THINK I'M PREGNANT!

A sort-of introduction by Denis Kitchen

I SHOULD BEGIN BY POINTING OUT THAT **COMIX BOOK** IS NOT A SLICK NEW YORK MAGAZINE. IT IS PRODUCED IN THE HEARTLAND OF AMERICA.

CARTOON FACTORY

SPECIAL DELIVERY!

BOX 7

LOCATION IS IMPORTANT. IN EDITING THIS MAGAZINE, I WANT TO AVOID THE ARTIFICIALITY OF THE EASTERN ESTABLISHMENT. I WANT TO STAY IN TOUCH WITH THE REAL WORLD.

WHY SHOULD WE MOVE TO NEW YORK? OUR RECEPTION IS JUST AS GOOD HERE!

RIGHT FROM THE BEGINNING I EMPHASIZED TO PUBLISHER STAN LEE THAT I WANTED **COMIX BOOK** TO BE A **DIFFERENT** KIND OF MAGAZINE...

BUT STAN, THESE OTHER COMICS APPEAL TO PIMPLY-FACED, MORONIC ADOLESCENTS!

'NUFF SAID, DEN... YOU WANT TO APPEAL TO PIMPLY-FACED INTELLECTUALS!

NO... I WANT TO APPEAL TO PIMPLY-FACED, MORONIC **ADULTS!**

WHAP!

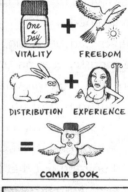

COMIX BOOK IS DESIGNED AS A HYBRID — A CROSS BETWEEN THE VITALITY AND FREEDOM OF UNDERGROUND COMIX... AND THE DISTRIBUTION AND EXPERIENCE OF AN ESTABLISHED COMPANY.

One a Day

VITALITY + FREEDOM

DISTRIBUTION + EXPERIENCE

= COMIX BOOK

ONCE WE SETTLED ON A FORMAT, STAN PROMISED ME TOTAL AUTONOMY.

OF COURSE THERE'S NO OBLIGATION, DEN, BUT **COMIX BOOK** MIGHT BE IDEAL TO SERIALIZE MY KOREAN WAR MEMOIRS... AND I WANT TO TRY MY HAND AT SOME OF THIS "UNDERGROUND" STUFF. I HAVE A SCRIPT FOR A DOPE-FIEND ANTI-HERO & HIS BARE-BREASTED SIDEKICK THAT I WANT YOU TO HAVE CRUMB PENCIL AND ARTIE SIMEK INK...

I PROCEEDED TO CONTACT AMERICA'S TOP UNDERGROUND CARTOONISTS...

FAR OUT, MAN!

Avante Garde!

RING!

AFTER CAREFULLY WEIGHING THE CULTURAL AND POLITICAL IMPLICATIONS, MOST ARTISTS AGREED TO PARTICIPATE.

LISTEN, MAN, WE'RE NOT GONNA SELL-OUT TO A GIANT, STRAIGHT, MADISON AVENUE PUBLISHING COMPANY!!

UH... HOW MUCH DOES IT PAY?

SOME "OLD PRO'S" WERE ALSO INVITED TO JOIN THE STAFF.

...EH?

AND REMEMBER: COMIX BOOK CARRIES NO ADVERTISING... SO OUR OPINIONS **CANNOT** BE BOUGHT!

RATS!

OIL LOBBY

Denis Kitchen, the cartoonist, explains in this one-page cartoon how *Comix Book* came to be. From *Comix Book* #1, 1974.

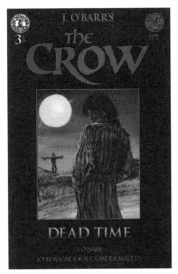

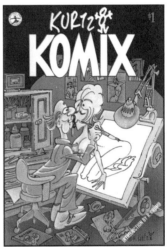

A selection of comic books from Kitchen Sink: *The Crow* (1996), *Snarf #7* (1977), *Father & Son #1* (1995), *Snoid Comics* (1980), *Energy Comics* (1980), *Kurtz Komix* (1976), *Death Rattle #2* (1995), *XYZ Comics* (1972), *Weird Trips* (1978).

63

The foreboding cover of *Snarf* #10, © 1987 by Will Elder.

In the middle 1970s, Krupp was offered a direct-solicitation comics distribution business for the entire Midwest. To accept would have meant a different business, with superhero comics sales the dominant factor. Kitchen backed out: "I had a passion for the alternative comics." (Capital City Distributors moved in.) If Kitchen Sink did anything mainstream, it was *Consumer Comix* in 1975, in cooperation with the Wisconsin Department of Consumer Affairs, on an OEO grant arranged shortly before President Nixon eradicated the federal agency. Distributed free to Wisconsin high school students, it highlighted corporate ripoffs like credit costs and was perhaps the highwater mark of a renewed La Follette progressivism gone visual. Kitchen also got involved in the *Fox River Patriot*, an alternative weekly considerably less dopey than the *Bugle* and more devoted to local history and ecology. Robert Crumb himself called it one of his favorite publications and sometimes provided art for covers.

Self-portraits by Poplaski, Kitchen, and Loft.

Kitchen Sink also became an arts novelties company, with buttons of current and once-famous artists, funny Christmas and greeting cards ("Congratulations on Your Big Dope Deal" and what may have been the first gay greeting card, drawn by Howard Cruse), lapel pins, T-shirts, posters, trading cards, candy bars, statuettes, and even retro metal signs. Best remembered of all these, inevitably, were a Crumb card series of blues musician-singers and a serigraph of Winters, California, undergoing steady visual degradation from farm days to sprawl, the kind of poster that took twelve passes through a silkscreen press to produce. For that matter, 3-D Comics, a fad of the middle 1950s that disappeared almost as suddenly as it had appeared, returned to life with Kitchen Sink several times over. Each book included cardboard glasses with red and green plastic lenses. Perhaps no one else would have considered it.

This was oddball stuff for sure. By the middle 1980s, Kitchen Sink had nevertheless evolved from underground comix (the *x* was in the process of being forgotten) into a broader comics operation, with its own offices and a line of classic reprints augmented by square-bound paperback books suitable for the usual bookstores. Not only was Kitchen the businessman the pride of the Princeton Chamber of Commerce but Kitchen Sink was a vital part of the alternative comics mainstream. Now less alternative than niche, comics were following the trend of alternative weekly tabloids with their own set of business decisions and generally reform-minded political takes on the local and national scene but mostly on entertainment.

Will Eisner's *The Spirit*. (See p. 68)

Denis Kitchen's cover for *Fox River Patriot*, #1, 1976.

Top left: Will Eisner's *A Contract with God and Other Tenement Stories,* republished by Kitchen Sink in 1985.

Top right: Harvey Kurtzman's *Jungle Book,* republished by Kitchen Sink in a deluxe hardcover version in 1986.

Left bottom: Crumb's artwork was used on the cover of *Fox River Patriot* #19, 1977.

Dope Comics, an early Kitchen Sink production, had given way, one might say, to *The Spirit* (an extended series of reprints with much original art and stories by Will Eisner added), to *Steve Canyon* comics by Milton Caniff, to *Li'l Abner* (also *Fearless Fosdick*, Al Capp's high point in satire), *Flash Gordon*, and several Harvey Kurtzman classics that had scarcely seen the light of day before disappearing from the public eye. Kitchen Sink had become, in effect, a comics *art* publisher, setting the path for others to follow.

In many ways, Denis Kitchen and his revolving staffs had prepared the way for the next steps in comics, steps that became clearer even as the cyclical crisis hit

Panel from *Maus* by Art Spiegelman, published first by Kitchen Sink, and later by Pantheon Books.

the comics trade again, and as the appearance of Art Spiegelman and Ben Katchor in the *New Yorker* magazine suggested the tilt that lay ahead. (Indeed, segments of *Maus* first appeared to a wider public in *Comix Book*, years before it won a Pulitzer prize for the author-artist.) One detail, however, should not be neglected: the ongoing fight against censorship. From a state where Republicans, Catholics, and assorted conservatives had not been notably successful since the 1950s, Kitchen himself led an anticensorship group of comics publishers and supporters with no particular political bent. They simply aimed their efforts, with the help of lawyers and sympathetic types, against the rollback perpetually threatened.

In all this, Kitchen was a frequent visitor to Madison and its comix denizens.

The Madison story meanwhile unfolds as a separate thread, with strands of fandom, superheroes including a certain Badger, and a lucrative distribution business that went bankrupt before Kitchen Sink did but with similar causes.

It's best to pick up the story on Monroe Street in 1975, where Bruce Ayres, son of a local progressive and boyhood pal of the son of famed UW historian William Appleman Williams, opened Capital City Comics. He and Steven Grant, a future comics scriptwriter, had brought out the first Madison-based comics fanzine a few years earlier, *The Vault of Mindless Fellowship*, a title sometimes punctuated by a final exclamation mark. *The Vault* didn't last long, but Bruce's store as the premier Wisconsin site for comics retail sales seems by now eternal, at least until

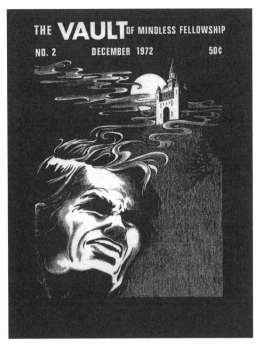

The Vault of Mindless Fellowship, published in 1972 by Wildwood Press. Cover by Mardy Ayres.

he retires. Madison's future scriptwriters, artists, and above all budding fans from across the state have found their way to the ever-loquacious owner and the store's overflowing stock for insight and encouragement.

Ayres knew everybody, and his circle of intimates definitely included the two collaborators who have hit it big commercially, writer Mike Baron and artist Steve Rude. Baron claims to have heard of Rude through the managing editor of the strikers' *Madison Press Connection* (and future comic scriptwriter) Dave Wagner, and that particular comics "connection" makes good sense: the paper's staff political cartoonist in its twenty-seven-month run was Mike Konopacki, another future comic artist of note.

Both Baron and Rude happened to be locals, the first taking classes at the University of Wisconsin and the second at Madison Area Technical College. They embarked professionally in 1981 with an ambitious sci-fi book, *Nexus*. It was very much in the EC Science Fiction tradition of the early 1950s, when comic art greats, including Harvey Kurtzman and Al Williamson, created galaxies of fantasy brought down to reality with references to the likely consequences of atomic war, very much on the minds of Americans in those dark years. Of course, the EC Comics were in color and, until the virtual suppression of comics done by

Capital City Comics, 1975-present.

69

Nexus, the Origin, © 2007 by Mike Baron and artist Steve Rude. Published by Rude Dude Productions.

a full staff of paid professionals and highly profitable. *Nexus* was in black and white for the first issues, with many cost-cutting features that insiders would immediately recognize as the stamp of the fanzine. The stories themselves tended toward the oblique or elliptical, the direction that postmodern mainstream comics were going, at least in the high artistic end of the trade.

Just two years later, in 1983, Baron brought out the first number of *Badger*, with art by Jeffrey Butler. Opening in northern Wales, circa AD 432, the comic finds a wizard in a tough spot. Somehow or other, he lands in the Mendota mental facility of the present, watched over by an exceptionally curvaceous case worker and joined by a former Badger football star / Vietnam vet who will become, in his alter-ego identity, you know who. Fairly typical superhero-style adventures follow.

Nexus and *Badger* were among the handful of books published by Capital Comics, sharing owners with the second-largest comics distribution company in the country, also based in Madison. Capital City Distribution, Inc., was an idea cooked up by local small businessmen who were also themselves comics fans, Milton Griepp and John Davis. The company lasted a little over sixteen years, and in that time it filled a gap left by the perpetual uncertainties of the comic book trade. By the mid-1980s, a whole new category of fan had been created, the organized collector, with trade

Nexus, from *The Origin,* © 2007 by Mike Baron & Steve Rude.

shows looking a bit like freak shows (costumed characters, elderly Jewish artists autographing their creations, seminaked babes sent by aggressive publishers, and a lot of adolescent guys with bad complexions, among assorted others) but also more than a little like authentic expressions of American popular culture. They were, in their odd enthusiasms, leading up to superhero-based Hollywood films, animation that would make the old Disney standards look pale, and leading also, of course, to comics-based video games. Unfortunately, all this wasn't enough to stave off another downturn of the commercial cycle that has been the bane of pulp trade: suddenly, comics sales would be falling, many storefronts could not survive new rent levels, and fans themselves seemed, at least for a moment, to weary of the whole thing. It happened one too many times for Capital City Distribution, although Griepp subsequently launched the insider business publication *ICv2*, which remains a major source of insight for comics dealers large and small. Capital Comics co-owner with Griepp, Madisonian Richard Bruning, ultimately became a DC senior vice president.

Badger #21, © 1987 by Mike Baron. Published by First Comics, Inc.

The artists and writers had meanwhile landed on their feet—by leaving town. Mike Baron went on to write for DC and Marvel, has won many industry awards, and is often rumored to be moving back to Wisconsin. Artist Steve Rude, in Dark Horse, First Comics, and elsewhere, has worked on big mainstream titles like *Spiderman* and even gone into movies. Steven Grant, another of the Capital crowd, joined Marvel in New York and, in his first big assignment, scored major in 1982 with *The Life of Pope John II*, "From his childhood in Poland to the Assassination Attempt." An unlikely assignment but done with great exactitude, it was actually colored by Marie Severin, ace colorist for EC in the early 1950s. Grant himself went on to modest success in mainstream comics, and is one of the more acute bloggers of the evolving art form.

The artistic drift through Madison continued undaunted between these commercial ups and downs. The *Daily Cardinal*'s leading cartoonist of the 1980s, James Sturm, was probably already looking toward better but also very different kinds of comic art. A few years after graduation from UW found him in New York, assisting Art Spiegelman in bringing out *Raw* magazine, the hottest avant-garde print-medium item with vernacular roots since American Dada circa 1920. Sturm, subsequently a comic artist of great renown (his genius creation and *Time* magazine's "Comic of the Year 2000," *The Golem's Mighty Swing*, tells about a traveling Jewish baseball team of the 1920s), was later to become the founder and director of the Center for Cartoon Studies in White River Junction, Vermont, and also of the National Association of Comic Arts Educators. True, he didn't really spend all that many years in Madison, but, true to Madison, Sturm became

The Golem's Mighty Swing, © 2001 by James Sturm.

an artist-educator after all. More important: Through Sturm, Madison was, at least vicariously, part of the *art* comics scene taking definitive shape in the wake of *New Yorker* showcasing of Spiegelman, Ben Katchor, Robert Crumb, and a very few other comic artists, now as prestigious as the magazine's premier cartoonists.

Zippy visits with the Cheese Mouse in Oakdale, Wisconsin. © 2006 by Bill Griffith.

The Adventures of Down and Out Dawg, © 1987 by James Sturm. Sturm drew the strip for the University of Wisconsin-Madison student newspaper *The Daily Cardinal.*

CHAPTER FOUR
ENDINGS AND NEW BEGINNINGS

In 2005–6, a traveling exhibit called "Masters of American Comics" showed the story of American comic art in a new light. Organized by the prestigious Hammer Museum and the Museum of Contemporary Art in Los Angeles, it was a bit more than a half century late in arriving but no less welcome. At last, the accomplishments of a formidable group of artists in the most widely read genre of visual literature (tabloid and comic book) have been recognized as bona-fide contributions to the art scene, rather than a source of interest mainly to overaged juveniles and obsessive trivia collectors. Those erstwhile underground comix giants Art Spiegelman and Robert Crumb were among the fifteen masters chosen for the exhibit. That Harvey Kurtzman, their single greatest individual inspiration, was another and two younger outspoken devotees of their own, Chris Ware and Gary Panter, round out the list completes the point that significant change has come along with recognition.

CRUMB   SPIEGELMAN   KURTZMAN   EISNER   HERRIMAN   CANIFF

Of the ten, only Frank O. King is a Wisconsin native. But Crumb, Spiegelman, and Kurtzman had seen plenty of action at Kitchen Sink, over the years, along with other now-acclaimed masters and Sink's popular artists-in-reprint, Will Eisner, George Herriman, and Milt Caniff.

Underground comix, in one way or another, were in this way also now very much implicated *historically* within the newly established comic art pantheon, for marketing reasons as much as aesthetic ones. The graphic novel has most definitely arrived in the chain stores and seems to be there to stay, a next "new thing" in

Underground Classics, © 2009 by James Danky and Denis Kitchen, cover art by Robert Crumb.

the fast-evolving world of publishing. The mega-million-dollar film productions based on comics characters, mostly animated, now underline the event of the year, the ComiCon International in San Diego, making it a Hollywood showplace for celebrities and money. Both graphic novel and film are connected in ways only beginning to be discovered by yet other media, emphatically including computer games.

It may be significant that the second stop of the "Masters" exhibit, the only tour site where anything like the full exhibit was offered, took place at the Milwaukee Art Museum in 2006. A bit of publicity attended to Frank King's Tomah connection (two color pages of his opened the lavish exhibit catalogue, and other comics were reprinted from vintage pages of the *Chicago Tribune*). But it must have seemed to many viewers that culture had been parachuted down to the nation's reputed flyover zone. It may be more significant that the first full underground comix exhibit (there have been a number of small-scale, underfunded events, and shows by particular artists' work, notably that of R. Crumb in San Francisco) opened at the Chazen Museum of Art on the UW-Madison campus in early May 2009.

Denis Kitchen had actually played a key role in the supply end of the exhibit, locating much obscure and otherwise unobtainable art (in addition to his own files, going back forty years, are his list of clients, including Crumb and the estates of Eisner, Kurtzman, and Capp) and a key role in selection for the Chazen exhibit. The latter's

Detail from *Gasoline Alley* by Frank O. King, as shown in the catalog for *Masters of American Comics*, © 2005 by Hammer Museum and the Museum of Contemporary Art, Los Angeles.

0co-organizer, James Danky, a retired Wisconsin Historical Society acquisitions archivist, has also been a scholar of the minority and alternative press for more than three decades. Here, in a sense, the saga of comics history has come back to Wisconsin full scale.

There is still another dimension, closer in a sense to the activist side of the Wisconsin progressive traditions but without abandoning the well-known penchant of the "Wisconsin School" of historians' compulsive documentation of the past. Comics here in Wisconsin, if anywhere, have reached a nonfiction crystallization within the first decade of the new century.

Late Days of Kitchen Sink

The nineties were an exceedingly odd time for comic art. *Raw* magazine, born in 1980, expired in 1991 with the anthological energy of its two editors, Art Spiegelman and Françoise Mouly. It never broke even. *Raw* had, however, accomplished mightily in stamping "art" in comics and impressing some mainstream critics. (They were probably more impressed to see Spiegelman in the *New Yorker*; he was by this time a semiregular, although he would quit in protest later on.) A large handful of young artists were beginning to make their mark in a number of genres (but more in the personal, autobiographical vein than any other), Joe Sacco to Peter Bagge, Joe Matt to Charles Burns and Richard Sala, not to mention Lynda Barry. Her Evergreen College pal Matt Groening's creations had meanwhile become the basis for *The Simpsons*, a revival of television animation long since faded in the Hanna-Barbera days of Yogi Bear and the Flintstones, but a great deal sharper, arguably the most politically acerbic commentary available anywhere on the follies of the self-congratulatory 1990s.

Logo design by Leslie Cabarga.

But comics, in their traditional format, were once more in bad trouble, this time in what might be seen in retrospect as the beginning of the end of the once-generic comic style, the thirty-two-pager with staple binding. And it was the end of Kitchen Sink's Wisconsin run: the operation merged with Tundra and moved to Northampton, Massachusetts, in 1993, collapsing entirely a half-dozen years later. During its first years out East, it encompassed Alan Moore as a scripter, published Crumb's *Kafka* and the definitive *R. Crumb Coffee Table Art Book* along with *Twisted Sisters*, an important women's anthology. But all that is another tale rather too far from our subject here.

The big story of Kitchen Sink's final years in Wisconsin was bound to be the *Grateful Dead Comix* snafu, a misalliance of comic art with rock hipsters and their agents, who were determined to present a drug-free image to young readers. Kitchen Sink's ever-growing list of other comic strip classics, brilliant and banal alike, hovered in the background. By the time of the move, the wholly unique *A Century of Women Cartoonists* was being planned, a major historical study by feminist comics pioneer Trina Robbins. A few years earlier, Kitchen Sink had published *Secret of San Saba*, by Jack Jaxon (aka Jackson), on Texas history, one section of what had become by that time arguably the boldest sustained venture of nonfiction comics to that time in the U.S. From another angle, *Kings in Disguise* (1990) by James Vance and Dan Burr was the fictional but true-to-era Depression saga of homeless males on the road, a *Grapes of Wrath* update. This was serious history in comics form and the beginning of a new phase for the next century.

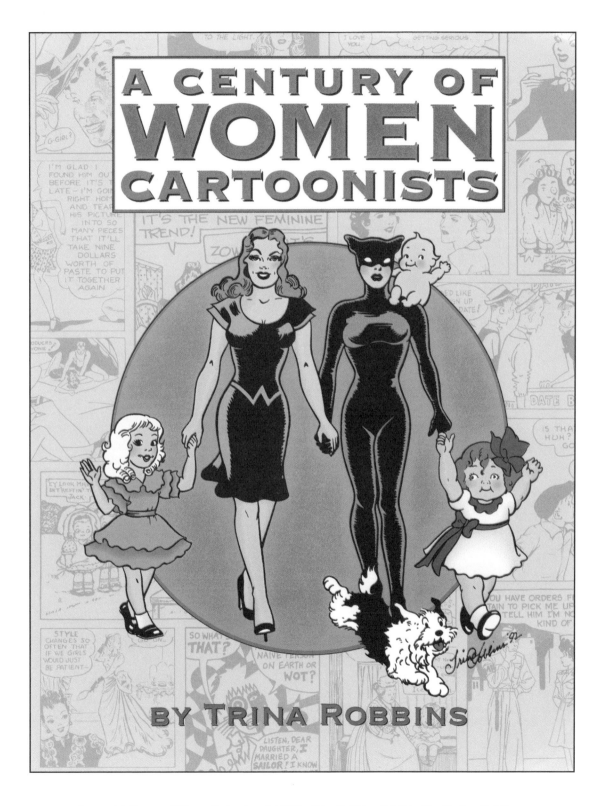

Cover of *A Century of Women Cartoonists,* © 1993 by Trina Robbins. Published by Kitchen Sink Press.

Excerpt from "Lulu Goes to Paris," © 1978 by Trina Robbins in *Snarf* #8. Published by Kitchen Sink Press.

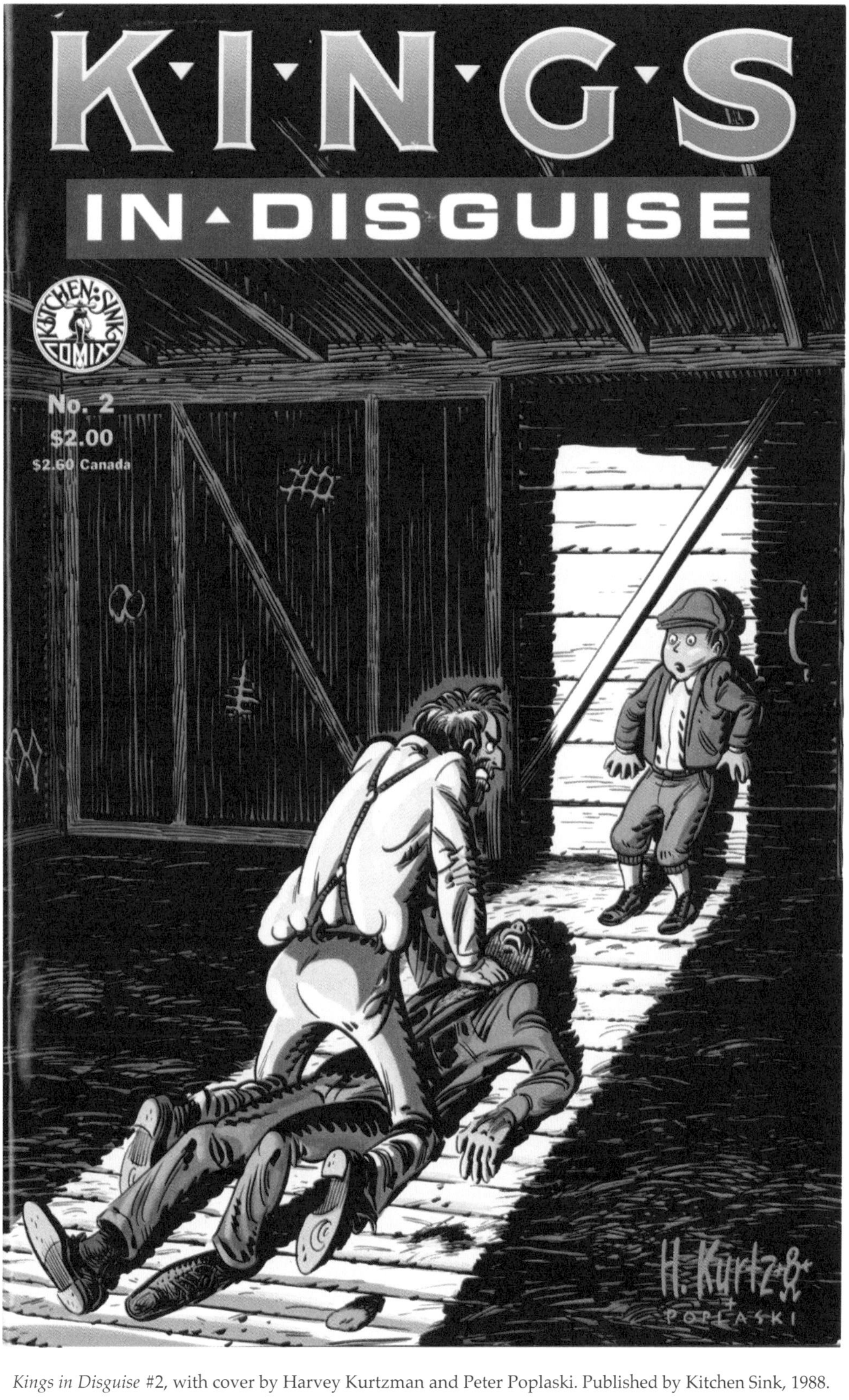
KINGS
IN DISGUISE
KITCHEN SINK COMIX
No. 2
$2.00
$2.60 Canada
H. Kurtz
POPLASKI

Kings in Disguise #2, with cover by Harvey Kurtzman and Peter Poplaski. Published by Kitchen Sink, 1988.

Excerpt from *Secret of San Saba: A Tale of Phantoms and Greed in the Spanish Southwest,* © 1989 by Jack Jackson (Jaxon). Published by Kitchen Sink Press.

In Madison and vicinity, meanwhile, other traditions were being refurbished. Tom Pomplun, a Madison local who grew up loving pulp fiction, took a job in the early 1990s as designer of *Rosebud*, a lit mag published in nearby Cambridge with occasional comics. After ten years there, Graphic Classics was born. The original Classics Illustrated, an immensely popular comic book series that ran from 1941 into the early 1960s, subsequently stumbled into cycles of collapse and small-scale revival. If the art had been stiff and the stories condensed to the point of driving professors and high school English teachers crazy, it was nevertheless an introduction to classic literature, such as *Huckleberry Finn* and *Leatherstocking Tales*.

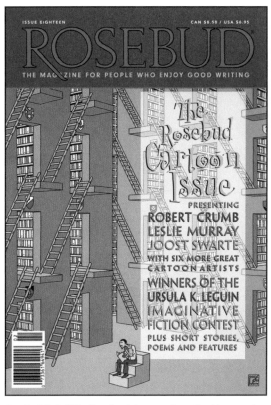

Rosebud #18, "The Rosebud Cartoon Issue" with cover by Joost Swarte. Published by Rosebud, Inc., 2000.

Pomplun's Graphic Classics lack the inside color pages, the art budget, and, most of all, the distribution of the original. But the art is often extremely good, an outlet for comic art genre professionals who rarely get the chance to do something serious, and the only chance for many of them to do literary adaptations, one of the fine arts of old-time illustrators. Classics is by now up to fifteen titles, with several revised and expanded along the way. Wisconsin favorites would naturally include the adaptations of H. P. Lovecraft, the horror writer of the 1930s–40s whose short stories and novelettes were reprinted by August Derleth's Arkham House Press in Sauk City, an old "free thought" center. (Derleth and the Sauk City freethinkers of the nineteenth century would have been proud of the Comic Book Legal Defense Fund, with Denis Kitchen and Milton Griepp on board, fighting censorship for the last twenty years or so.)

There are, naturally, still other players and games within the diversity of Wisconsin's comics scene. Among them is this volume's own designer, Steve Chappell, a Stevens Point native who transplanted to Madison in the 1980s and became an outstanding

Derleth at home in Sauk City, Wisconsin with his comics collection. From the archives of the August Derleth Society.

Excerpts and covers from the *Graphic Classics* series, edited by Tom Pomplun. From left to right, covers by Esao Andrews, George Sellas, and Steven Cerio. Published by Eureka Productions. Page drawn by Rick Geary, from Edgar Allan Poe's *Tell-Tale Heart*.

Excerpt from "The Terrible Old Man," © 2002 by Onsmith Jeremi, from *Graphic Classics,*
H.P. Lovecraft. Published by Eureka Productions. Cover by Todd Schorr.

85

Cover and excerpt from *Rosebud* #24, "Conflagration," © 1997 by Skip Williamson.

THE WAR WAS AN ECCLESIAST-
ICAL EX-
PERIENCE.

THE IMMOLATION WAS
EXCITING AND
OMNIPOTENT. AND
THEY CAME TO LOVE
THEIR WORK.

HOWITZERS AND GRENADES SPLATTERING FLESH AND SPLINTERING BONE WERE A
CORROBORATION OF GOD'S RANDOM ANGER. THEY WERE PARTICIPANTS IN A GRISLY DIVINITY.

THE INCONTROVERTIBLE
SLAUGHTER WAS AT ONCE INDIS-
CRIMINATE YET OF CELESTIAL
DESIGN.

THE ANGEL OF DEATH WAS STILL AN ANGEL.

END

Cover and excerpt from *Stark Reality*, "I Can Only Imagine," © 1997 by Steve Chappell. Published by Rolling Tire Productions.

graphic artist. Comic books are strictly a sideline for Chappell, but his self-published *Stark Reality* ("For Spacious Thinkers Only!") is both delightfully quirky and deeply committed to the saga of leftwing popular culture in town. Likewise, on Madison's East Side, Alex Wood's Wildwood Productions has begun to print serigraphs of Robert Crumb's comic panels and small-run productions of a recent Crumb series, *Mystic Funnies*.

P. S. Mueller, more cartoonist than comic strip artist, is one of those rare Wisconsin comics talents who has stayed in Madison. His pungent wit is unceasing and his work seems to appear almost everywhere--right up to the present day.

UW grad and Madison homeboy John Kovalic, an escapee for other parts, edits what has become a prize-winning "game related periodical" known by the ironic knockoff title *Dork Tower* and featuring characters' lives in Mud Bay, Wisconsin (aka Madison). For the past decade it's been on the Web and, less often, in printed form and remains as dorky as ever. Kovalic's comics, on-line and published, are matched by his designs present on popular video games.

Mystic Funnies #1, © 1997 by Robert Crumb. Published in Madison, Wisconsin, by Alex Wood with the assistance of Jesse Crumb and Tom Pomplun.

The (Re)birth of Nonfiction Comics

Nonfiction comics have existed almost since the dawn of the comic strip—if advertising and its chamber of commerce variant, local boosterism, can be considered nonfiction. The earliest of separately published Wisconsin cartoon (if not comic) books may be *A Cartoon History of Green County* (c. 1930), made up of reprinted panels from a local daily. Businesses with the wherewithal followed the success of early comic books with eight-to-sixteen-page advertising booklets during the 1930s–50s, a counterpart to the occasional, highly varnished, illustrated corporate history. Anticommunist comics, purported to be nonfiction but much along the science fiction (or fantasy) line, hit the presses in cold war days, though never actually published in Joe McCarthy's own territory.

Alternative comics, leaning leftward, produced some great muckraking and popularization, not only

Corporate Crime Comics, © 1979 Kitchen Sink Press. Cover by Pete Poplaski.

89

Dork Tower #14, © 2001 by John Kovalic. Published by Dork Storm Press.

Excerpt from "Head Case," © 1989 by P. S. Mueller in *Snarf* #11. Published by Kitchen Sink Press. Cover by Rand Holmes.

Wobblies!, © 2005 by Paul Buhle, and various artists. Cover by Nicole Schulman.

a few Kitchen Sink titles (notably *Corporate Crime Comics*) but the highly successful books by Larry Gonick, exploring science subjects of various types. *World War 3 Illustrated*, more or less annual since 1978, has been an anthological project for radical observations, some historical, most current-day tales of war, neocolonial economics, residential gentrification, and assorted species of corporate exploitation and brutality. It could also be argued that the entirety of prize-winning American Splendor comics scripted by Harvey Pekar and drawn by many hands has been an epic in nonfiction (as well as leading to an award-winning film of the same title in 2002). But only after the appearance of

Excerpt from *Wobblies!*, "Time to dis-Organize," © 2004 by Jay Kinney.

92

Spiegelman's two-volume oral history interpretation, *Maus*, along with Joe Sacco's Baltic War narratives, and then only in the new century, did a nonfiction of a new kind see a consolidation of sorts.

Comic art can, of course, tell a very different kind of history distinct from oral history, personal history, or family history and thereby closer to the historian's familiar art. The work of Jaxon was the outstanding case in point. Looking for a twenty-first-century counterpart would lead inexorably to *Wobblies! A Graphic History*, released on the 2005 centenary of the Industrial Workers of the World (IWW). It was, taken altogether, an effort to tell labor's story in a different way, at once closer to cultural history, the emerging scholarly field of "Border Studies," and transnationalism than to older versions of working-class saga. One of the centers of a modest IWW revival from the 1980s onward (Lakeside Press, a Wobbly job shop on Williamson Street for decades, prints posters for political and cultural events), Madison was a natural place for the artist-personal connections making

a book like this possible. I was coeditor and becoming a Madisonian again; artist Mike Konopacki, raised in Manitowoc, had arrived in town in the early 1970s and never left; nor had fellow contributor Sue Simensky Bietala abandoned her adopted Milwaukee. Wobbly woodcut artist Carlos Cortez, who died while the book was in production, claimed to have been the first Mexican American ever born in Milwaukee, son of a rambling Wobbly and a local German American woman. Cortez served as inspiration for other artists' commitment to labor's globalism and in particular the book's Mexican American tilt.

Out of *Wobblies!* more volumes of the nonfiction genre grew, kin in their historical content and in their artistic quality. *A Dangerous Woman*, the graphic biography of Emma Goldman by erstwhile Madisonian Sharon Rudahl appeared in 2007 and *Students for a Democratic Society: A Graphic History* a year later, in the hands of the same editor. Emma, the notorious anarchist, had never made it to

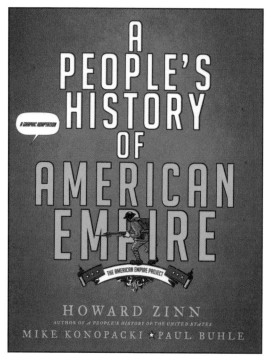

A People's History of American Empire, © 2008 by Zinn, Konopacki, and Buhle.

Madison, but SDS had one of its strongest branches there during the latter half of the 1960s, and the saga of the New Left emerges here (along with stories from Austin, Iowa City, Manhattan, and elsewhere) with the Dow riot of 1967 (police and university administrators versus antiwar students), the meetings with intellectual activists on campus and beyond, and the creation of *Radical America Komiks*, a Madison story in itself. Nick Thorkelson is notable among this book's artists, and in that sense the nonfiction genre followed Thorkelson and Jim O'Brien's earlier *Underhanded History of America*.

The next noteworthy event was the publication of *A People's History of American Empire* (2008), a volume of nonfiction comics, somewhat loosely based on Howard Zinn's *People's History of the United States*, that became a bestseller. Its editor, myself, scriptwriter Dave Wagner, *Capital Times* political cartoonist Mike Konopacki, and his assistant on the book, Kathy Wilkes, are all Madisonians.

The term "loosely," inevitable for any comic adaptation, is especially applicable here. The additional material comes from two quarters: first, the scholarship on American empire by the great Madison historian William Appleman Williams; and second, the scholarship on popular culture's interracial creativity in the rock 'n roll age by Madison Ph.D. and former *Cultural Correspondence* editor George Lipsitz, thereafter a dean of American Studies. Further volumes in a historical, nonfiction series edited by myself—biographies of Che Guevara and Isadora

The Pullman Strike

GEORGE PULLMAN TRIED TO SOLVE HIS LABOR PROBLEMS BY BUILDING A COMPANY TOWN OUTSIDE CHICAGO THAT HE NAMED AFTER HIMSELF. HE CHARGED HIGH RENTS AND CONTROLLED EVERY ASPECT OF HIS WORKERS' LIVES. HE CALLED THEM "MY CHILDREN." IT WAS A VERSION OF THE INDIAN RESERVATION SYSTEM. ON MAY 11, 1894, CHICAGO WORKERS OF THE *PULLMAN PALACE CAR COMPANY* STRUCK TO PROTEST WAGE CUTS AND THE FIRING OF UNION REPRESENTATIVES.

Two-page excerpt from *A People's History of American Empire*, "The Pullman Strike," © 2008 by Zinn, Konopacki, and Buhle.

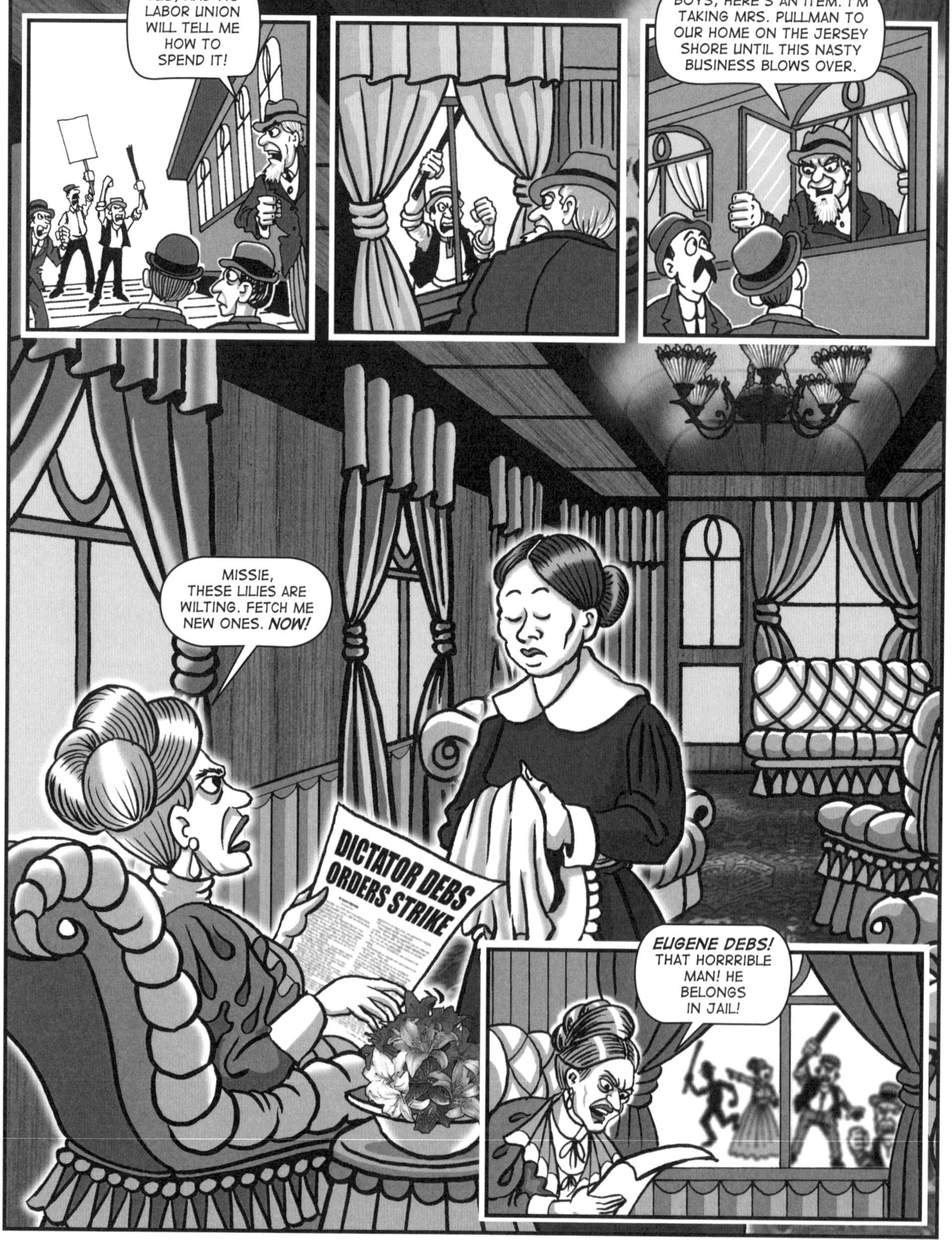
YES, AND NO LABOR UNION WILL TELL ME HOW TO SPEND IT!
BOYS, HERE'S AN ITEM. I'M TAKING MRS. PULLMAN TO OUR HOME ON THE JERSEY SHORE UNTIL THIS NASTY BUSINESS BLOWS OVER.
MISSIE, THESE LILIES ARE WILTING. FETCH ME NEW ONES. *NOW!*
DICTATOR DEBS ORDERS STRIKE
EUGENE DEBS! THAT HORRRIBLE MAN! HE BELONGS IN JAIL!

Cover of *Che,* © 2008 by Spain Rodriguez. Published by Verso.

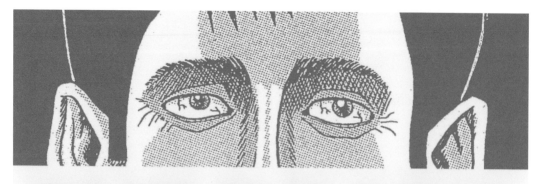

THE BEATS
A Graphic History

Text by Harvey Pekar, Nancy Peters, Penelope Rosemont, Joyce Brabner, and Trina Robbins
Edited by Paul Buhle
Art by Ed Piskor, Jay Kinney, Nick Thorkelson, Summer McClinton, Peter Kuper, Mary Fleener, Jerome Neukirch, Anne Timmons, Gary Dumm, Lance Tooks, and Jeffrey Lewis

Cover of *The Beats*, © 2009 by Pekar, Piskor, and Buhle. Published by Hill and Wang.

Three-page excerpt from *Students for a Democatic Society, A Graphic History*, "Madison Strike Riot," © 2008 by Paul Buhle and Gary Dumm. Published by Hill and Wang.

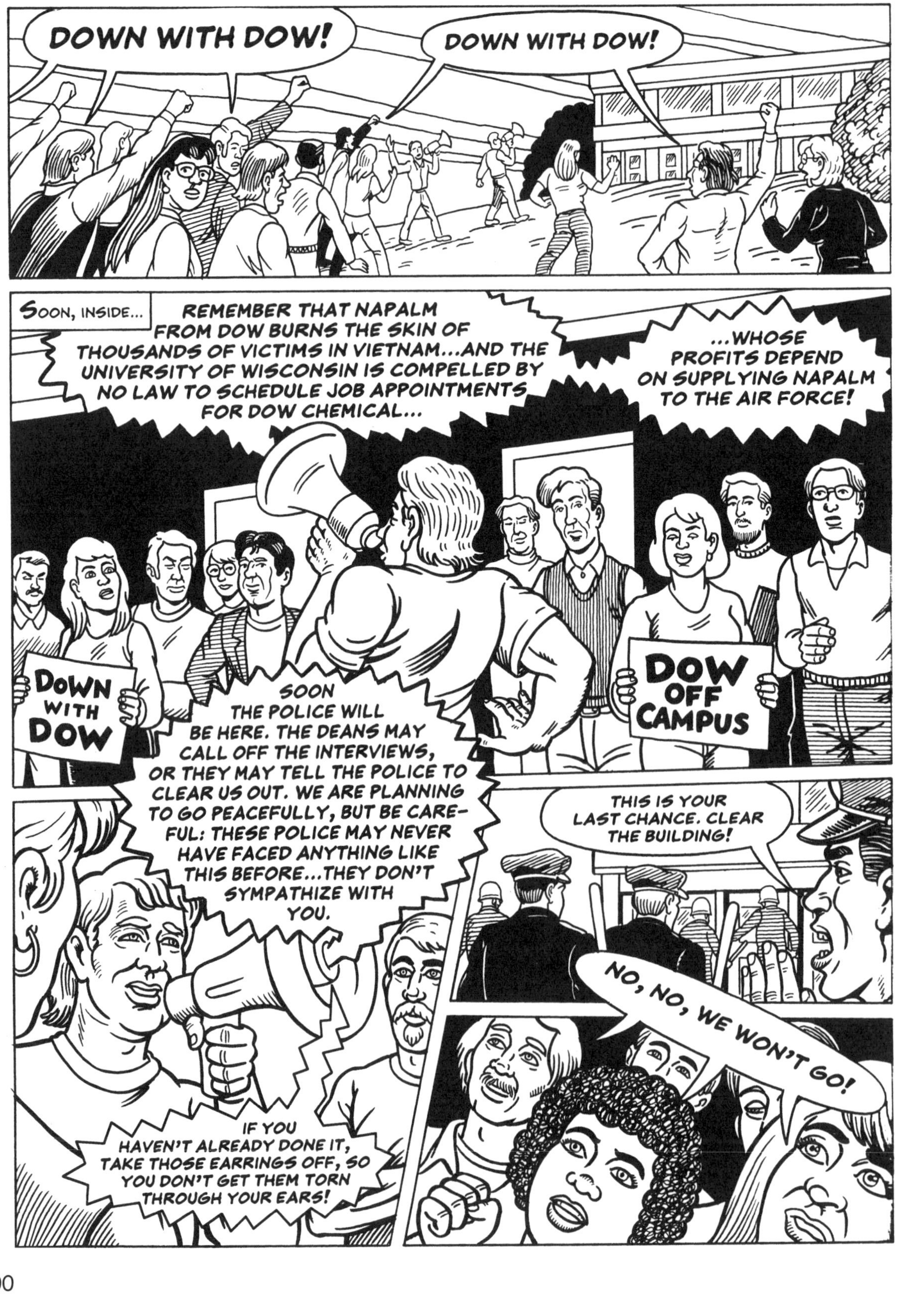
DOWN WITH DOW!
DOWN WITH DOW!
SOON, INSIDE...
REMEMBER THAT NAPALM FROM DOW BURNS THE SKIN OF THOUSANDS OF VICTIMS IN VIETNAM...AND THE UNIVERSITY OF WISCONSIN IS COMPELLED BY NO LAW TO SCHEDULE JOB APPOINTMENTS FOR DOW CHEMICAL...
...WHOSE PROFITS DEPEND ON SUPPLYING NAPALM TO THE AIR FORCE!
DOWN WITH DOW
DOW OFF CAMPUS
SOON THE POLICE WILL BE HERE. THE DEANS MAY CALL OFF THE INTERVIEWS, OR THEY MAY TELL THE POLICE TO CLEAR US OUT. WE ARE PLANNING TO GO PEACEFULLY, BUT BE CARE-FUL: THESE POLICE MAY NEVER HAVE FACED ANYTHING LIKE THIS BEFORE...THEY DON'T SYMPATHIZE WITH YOU.
IF YOU HAVEN'T ALREADY DONE IT, TAKE THOSE EARRINGS OFF, SO YOU DON'T GET THEM TORN THROUGH YOUR EARS!
THIS IS YOUR LAST CHANCE. CLEAR THE BUILDING!
NO, NO, WE WON'T GO!

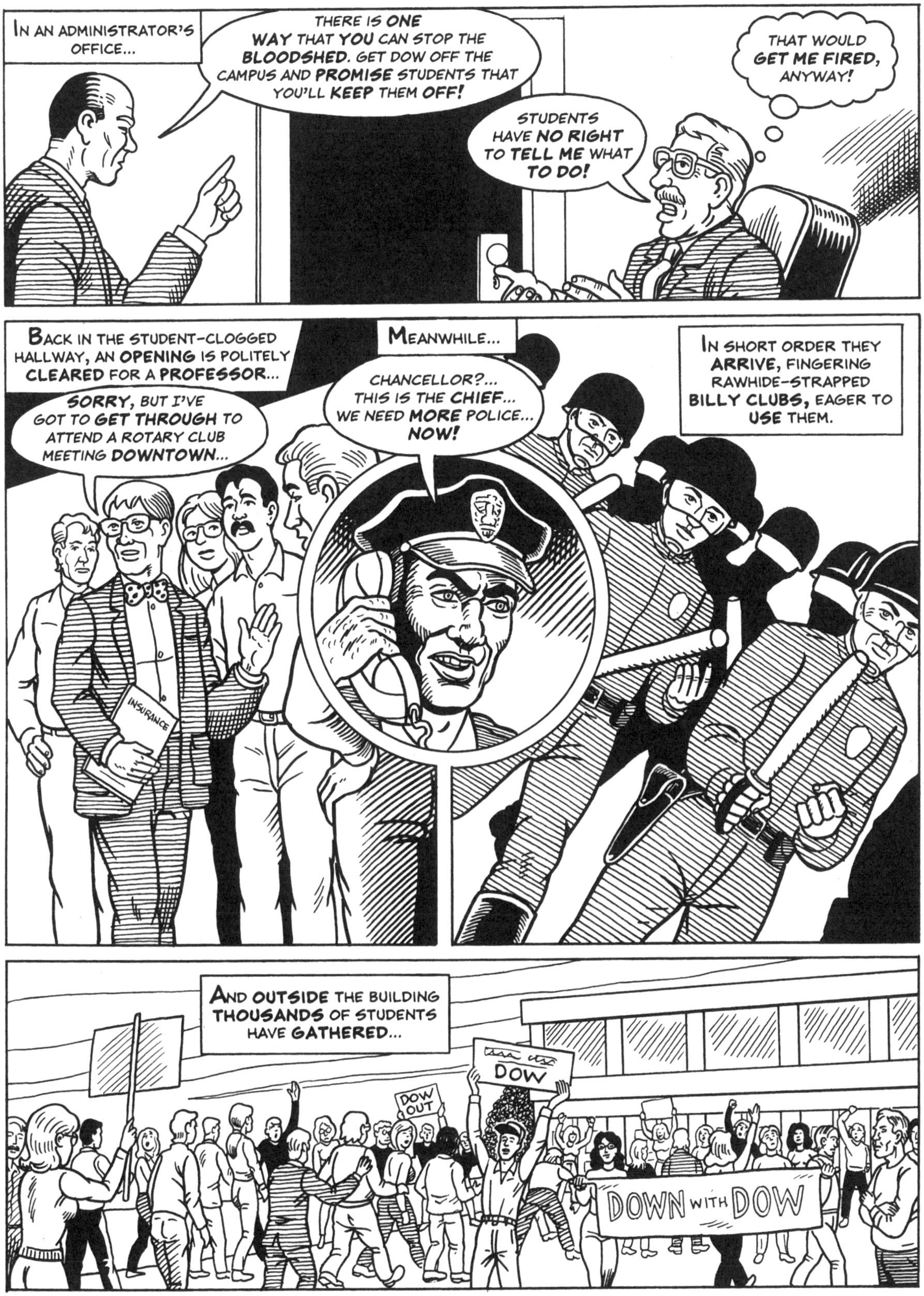
IN AN ADMINISTRATOR'S OFFICE...
THERE IS ONE WAY THAT YOU CAN STOP THE BLOODSHED. GET DOW OFF THE CAMPUS AND PROMISE STUDENTS THAT YOU'LL KEEP THEM OFF!
STUDENTS HAVE NO RIGHT TO TELL ME WHAT TO DO!
THAT WOULD GET ME FIRED, ANYWAY!
BACK IN THE STUDENT-CLOGGED HALLWAY, AN OPENING IS POLITELY CLEARED FOR A PROFESSOR...
SORRY, BUT I'VE GOT TO GET THROUGH TO ATTEND A ROTARY CLUB MEETING DOWNTOWN...
INSURANCE
MEANWHILE...
CHANCELLOR?... THIS IS THE CHIEF... WE NEED MORE POLICE... NOW!
IN SHORT ORDER THEY ARRIVE, FINGERING RAWHIDE-STRAPPED BILLY CLUBS, EAGER TO USE THEM.
AND OUTSIDE THE BUILDING THOUSANDS OF STUDENTS HAVE GATHERED...
DOW
DOW OUT
DOWN with DOW

ADAPTED BY
HARVEY PEKAR

EDITED BY
PAUL BUHLE

"It's the essence of Studs, seen from a new angle." —ROGER EBERT

Studs Terkel's

WORKING

a graphic adaptation

Cover of *Studs Terkel's Working,* © 2009 by Pekar, Buhle, and various artists. Published by New Press. Cover by Sabrina Jones.

NICK SALERNO, GARBAGEMAN

He has been driving a city garbage truck for eighteen years. He is forty-one, married, and has three daughters. He works a forty-hour, five-day week with occasional overtime. He has a crew of three laborers.

I usually get up at five-fifteen.

I get to the city parking lot, you check the oil, your water level, then proceed to the ward yard. You meet the men, we pick up our work sheet.

You get up just like the milkman's horse, you get used to it. If you remember the milkman's horse, all he had to do was whistle and whooshhh! That's it.
He just knew where to stop, didn't he?

You pull up until you finish the alley. Usually thirty homes on each side. You have thirty stops in our alley. I have nineteen alleys a week. They're called units.

Sometimes I can't finish 'em, that's how heavy they are, this being an old neighborhood.

I'll sit there until they pick this one stop. You got different thoughts. Maybe you got a problem at home. Maybe one of your children aren't feeling too good. Like my second one. She's got a problem with her homework. Am I doin' the right thing with her? Pressing her a little bit with math.

Or you read the paper. You always daydream.

Two-page excerpt from *Studs Terkel's Working*, "Nick Salerno, Garbageman," © 2009 by Nick Thorkelson. Published by New Press.

We've got spotters now, it's new (laughs). They're riding around in unmarked cars. They turn you in for stopping for coffee. I can't see that.

If you have a coffee break in the alley it's just using a little psychology. You'll get more out of them. But if you're watched continually, you're gonna lay down. There's definitely more watching today, because there was a lot of layin' down on the job. Truthfully I'd just as soon put in my eight hours a day as easy as possible. It's hard enough comin' to work.

I got a good crew, we get along together, but we have our days.

If you're driving all day you get tired. By the time you get home, fighting the traffic, you'd just like to relax a little bit. But there's always something around the house, you can get home one night and find your kid threw something in the toilet and you gotta shut your mind and take the toilet apart (laughs).

My wife drives so she does most of the shopping. That was my biggest complaint. So now this job is off my hands, I look forward to the weekends, I get in a little golf.

People ask what I do, I say, I drive a garbage truck for the city. They call you G-man or, "How's business, picking up?" Just the standard.... Or sanitary engineer. I have nothing to be ashamed of. I put in my eight hours. We make a pretty good salary. I feel I earn my money. I can go anywhere I want. I conduct myself as a gentleman anyplace I go.

My wife is happy, this is the big thing. She doesn't look down at me.

They made a crack to my children in school. My kids would just love to see me do something else. I tell'm, "Honey, this is a good job. There's nothing to be ashamed of. We're not stealin' the money. You have everything you need." I don't like my salary compared to anyone else's. I don't like to hear that we're makin' more than a schoolteacher. A schoolteacher should get more money, but

don't take it away from me.

NICK THORKELSON

Duncan, an adaptation of Studs Terkel, and a popular survey, *The Beats*—were not specifically Wisconsin in artists, but contained a recurring theme that oldtime and even recent Madisonians would recognize. This was the avant-garde, radical, but also radically heterodox, view of the past and the great personalities in it. Culture heroes might be ordinary people, and great dancers figured as large as guerilla fighters.

These things do seem to circle in upon themselves suspiciously and we might best close the historical narrative with the return of a very different artist, Lynda Barry, often considered to be the largest Badger comics talent since the early work of Frank King. Barry was born in 1956 in Richland Center, though she was moved during childhood to the state of Washington—the Midwest of the Northwest, some say. She went to the experimental Evergreen State College, where her friend (and fellow cartoonist) Matt Groening published some of her work in the school paper, not bothering to mention his intentions to the overly modest Barry. She moved on to Seattle,

Excerpt from *The! Greatest! of! Marlys!*, © 2000 by Lynda Barry.

where her work was picked up by the *Chicago Reader* in 1979, and during the Reagan Years she steadily emerged as a fresh talent utterly unique in her artistic approach and narrative, at the same time militantly political in her resistance to the rightwing drift of the country and dominant culture. After a spell in Chicago, in 2008 she moved to the village of Footville, west of Janesville in southern Wisconsin, with her husband, a naturalist.

Barry manages to capture the anxiety of preteens who feel like losers but are really the bohemians of a coming generation, uninterested in making it, compelled to explore alternatives just to survive psychically. There are plenty of jokes and discoveries about themselves, about the world immediately around them and the world further away, but the treatment of childhood as something less than nurturing, let alone idyllic, has an understandably wide appeal. It denies American collective denial, notably in an era when new gadgets are said to make life more interesting and even fulfilling if only the global ecology and the domestic

Two-page excerpt from *What It Is*, © 2008 by Lynda Barry. Published by Drawn & Quarterly, Montreal, Quebec.

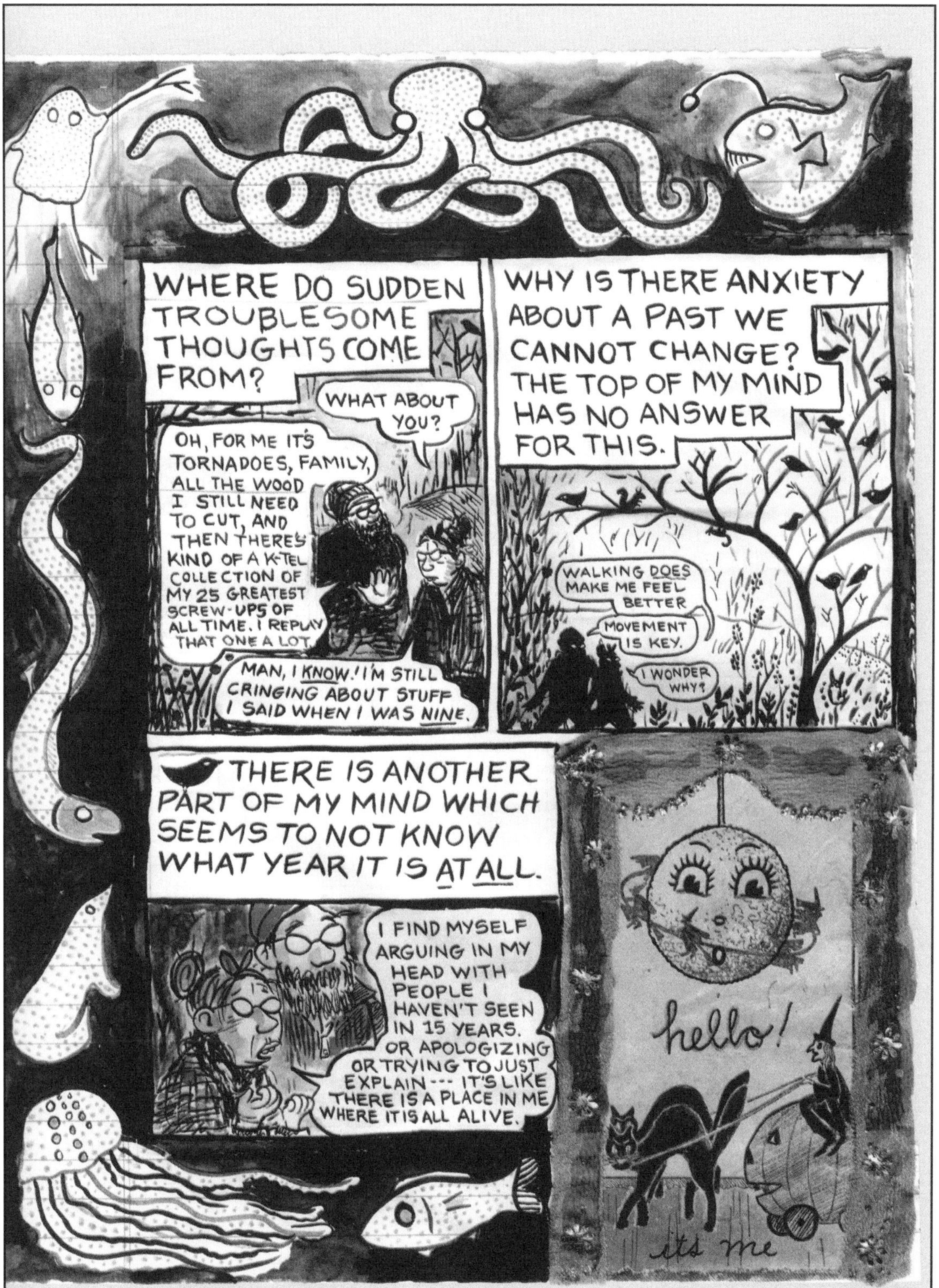
WHERE DO SUDDEN TROUBLESOME THOUGHTS COME FROM?
WHAT ABOUT YOU?
OH, FOR ME IT'S TORNADOES, FAMILY, ALL THE WOOD I STILL NEED TO CUT, AND THEN THERE'S KIND OF A K-TEL COLLECTION OF MY 25 GREATEST SCREW-UPS OF ALL TIME. I REPLAY THAT ONE A LOT.
MAN, I KNOW! I'M STILL CRINGING ABOUT STUFF I SAID WHEN I WAS NINE.
WHY IS THERE ANXIETY ABOUT A PAST WE CANNOT CHANGE? THE TOP OF MY MIND HAS NO ANSWER FOR THIS.
WALKING DOES MAKE ME FEEL BETTER
MOVEMENT IS KEY.
I WONDER WHY?
THERE IS ANOTHER PART OF MY MIND WHICH SEEMS TO NOT KNOW WHAT YEAR IT IS AT ALL.
I FIND MYSELF ARGUING IN MY HEAD WITH PEOPLE I HAVEN'T SEEN IN 15 YEARS. OR APOLOGIZING OR TRYING TO JUST EXPLAIN--- IT'S LIKE THERE IS A PLACE IN ME WHERE IT IS ALL ALIVE.
hello!
it's me
6

economy don't collapse.

Visually, a move away from pen-work in the middle 1980s (Barry claimed it hurt her wrist) to brush may have been one of the great comic art discoveries since a young Harvey Kurtzman picked up a brush for his fine comics work in the early 1940s. Working in color as only a handful of comic artists are fortunate enough to be able to do (more of them manage it in children's books, as a day job), Barry does something unanticipated with comic art; she restyles it. In that sense, she has played no small role in bringing a new kind of comic art into existence.

The story of comics in Wisconsin is obviously not over. Young artists are breaking into the superhero mainstream and its margins, among other developments. But the latest moment is, for a history-minded place, not surprisingly a piece of recuperated history, the Chazen Museum's underground comix exhibit and accompanying catalogue as totem of things past and perhaps also of things to come. Why Madison? Perhaps because too many smaller efforts have been made in the Bay Area and Seattle, perhaps because New York can never really be a sentimental spot for comix. But no doubt the meaning of place has more than a little to do with the legacy of Princeton, Wisconsin, as a site of comics history understood as part of a continuing comic-art development, with a future resting firmly upon the past. One could argue that something Madisonian had spread or perhaps been overtaken by cultural moods and ecological projects across large parts of the state. Then again, Madison had pointed toward the future as an underground city, a fixture as well as a Wisconsin type. Comic art had to come from somewhere besides New York and the Bay Area, and Wisconsin has contributed more than its share.

Zippy chats with public sculpture in Sparta, Wisconsin. © 2000 by Bill Griffith.

SELECTED BIBLIOGRAPHY

Paul Buhle, ed., *Popular Culture in America*. Minneapolis: University of Minnesota Press, 1990.

Steve Chappell, *Stark Reality*. Madison: Rolling Tire Productions, 1997.

From Aargh! To Zap! Harvey Kurtzman's Visual History of the Comics. New York: Prentice Hall, 1991.

David Hajdu, *The Ten-Cent Plague: The Great Comic-Book Scare and How it Changed America*. New York: Farrar, Straus and Giroux, 2008.

Denis Kitchen and Paul Buhle, *The Art of Harvey Kurtzman*. New York: Abrams, 2009.

David Kunzle, *Father of the Comic Strip, Rodolphe Töpffer*. Jackson: University Press of Mississippi, 2007.

Masters of American Comics. Edited by John Carlin, Paul Karasik, and Brian Walker. Los Angeles and New Haven: The Hammer Museum, the Museum of Contemporary Art, Los Angeles, and Yale University Press, 2005.

Patrick Rosenkrantz, *Rebel Visions: The Underground Comix Revolution*, 1963-1975. Seattle: Fantagraphic Books, 2002.

Dave Schreiner, *Kitchen Sink Press, The First 25 Years*. Northampton: Kitchen Sink Press, 1994.

Dez Skinn, *Comix: The Underground Revolution*. New York: Thunder's Mouth Press, 2004.

Walt and Skeezix by Frank O. King, 1921-1922. Montreal: Drawn and Quarterly, 2002. Introduction by Jeet Heer. Seattle: Fantagraphic Books, 2002.

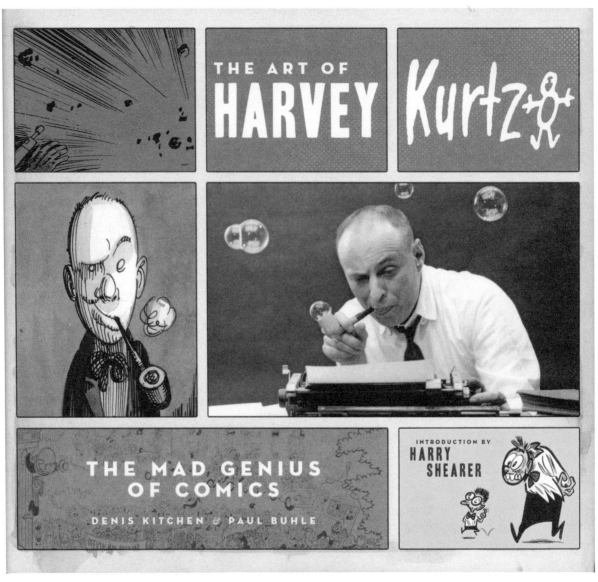

The Art of Harvey Kurtzman, The Mad Genius of Comics, © 2009 by Denis Kitchen and Paul Buhle. Published by Abrams ComicArts.

Zippy stops back in Sparta, Wisconsin. He likes Sparta. © 2008 by Bill Griffith.

ADDITIONAL COPYRIGHT & ART CREDITS

Page 7: Hieronymus Bosch, detail from *The Garden of Earthly Delights*, 1503. Oil on board, Museo del Prado, Madrid.

Page 10: T. E. Powers, *It Might Have Been Worse!*, © 1911. Reprinted from *Art Out of Time, Unknown Comics Visionaries, 1900-1969*, © 2006 by Dan Nadel, published by Harry N. Abrams.

Page 11: Art Young, cover of *The Masses*, November 1914. Provided by Department of Special Collections, Memorial Library, University of Wisconsin-Madison.

Page 14: Sidney Smith, *The Gumps*, 1917. Reprinted from *The Comics Before 1945*, © 2004 by Brian Walker, published by Harry N. Abrams.

Page 15: Sidney Smith, *The Gumps*, 1924. Reprinted from *The Smithsonian Collection of Newspaper Comics*, © 1984 by Bill Blackbeard and Martin Williams, co-published by Smithsonian Institution and Harry N. Abrams.

Page 16: Frank O. King, *Bobby Make-Believe*, 1916. Barnacle Press, an on-line resource of classic comics, mostly from the turn of the century through the 1930s. www.barnaclepress.com

Pages 17 and 18: Frank O. King, *Gasoline Alley*, 1924. Reprinted from *Masters of American Comics*, © 2005 by the Hammer Museum and the Museum of Contemporary Art of Los Angeles.

Pages 23 and 24: Gerald Gregg, Dell covers for *The Dark Device*, and *The Broken Vase*. Reprinted from an article by Piet Schreuders, "Gerald Gregg and the Dell Mapbacks," *Illustration*, 3 (February 2004), pp. 55-67.

Page 27: *Feds 'N' Heads Comics*, © 1968 by Gilbert Shelton, published by Print Mint.

Page 34: Harvey Kurtzman, *Two-Fisted Tales* #25. Originally published in 1951 by Fables Publishing Co., Inc. *Tales Calculated to Drive You Mad* #4, 1953, published by EC Comics.

Page 55: Ernie Bushmiller, *Nancy Eats Food*. Published in 1989 by Kitchen Sink Press, edited by James Kitchen.

Page 56: *The Crush*, © 1987 by Alison Bechdel, from *Gay Comix* #10. Cover art by Peter Keane, © 1987 Robert Triptow.

Page 63: *The Crow* (1996), cover by Alexander Maleev; *Snarf* #7 (1977), cover by Art Spiegelman; *Father & Son* #1 (1995), cover by Jeff Nicholson; *Snoid Comics* (1980), cover by R. Crumb; *Energy Comics* (1980), cover by Denis Kitchen; *Kurtz Komix* (1976), cover by Harvey Kurtzman; *Death Rattle* #2 (1995), cover by Brian Biggs;

XYZ Comics (1972), cover by R. Crumb; *Weird Trips* (1978), cover by William Stout.

Page 65: image of *The Spirit,* © 1951 by Will Eisner and republished in 1990 on the cover of *The Spirit* #66 by Kitchen Sink Press.

Page 75: *Self-Loathing Comics #2,* © 1997 by R. Crumb and others, Kitchen Sink Press; *Maus II, And Here My Troubles Began,* © 1986 by Art Spiegelman, Pantheon Books; *Kurtz Komix,* © 1976 by Harvey Kurtzman, Kitchen Sink Press; *The Spirit #66,* © 1990 by Will Eisner, Kitchen Sink Press; *Krazy Kat,* © 1939 by George Herriman, reprinted in *Masters of American Comics,* © 2005 by the Hammer Museum and the Museum of Contemporary Art of Los Angeles; *Terry and the Pirates,* © 1940 by Milton Caniff, reprinted in *Masters of American Comics,* © 2005 by the Hammer Museum and the Museum of Contemporary Art of Los Angeles.

Page 84: excerpts and covers from the *Graphic Classics* series, edited by Tom Pomplun. Published by Eureka Productions. *O. Henry,* "The Ransom of Red Chief," © 2005 Esao Andrews; *Mark Twain,* "Tom Sawyer Abroad," © 2007 George Sellas; *Ambrose Bierce,* "Selections from The Devil's Dictionary," © 2008 Steven Cerio; *Edgar Allan Poe,* "Tell-Tale Heart," © 2004 Rick Geary.

Page 92: *Wobblies! A Graphic History of the Industrial Workers of the World,* © 2005 by the individual contributors. Published by Verso.

Page 105: *The! Greatest! of! Marlys!,* © 2000 by Lynda Barry. Published by Sasquatch Books.

Zippy visits the Yummy Buffet in Madison, Wisconsin (on Gilman near State). © 2005 by Bill Griffith.

INDEX

Page numbers for illustrations are in **boldface**.

Zippy visits with the Cheeseburger Mouse in Kenosha, Wisconsin. © 2000 by Bill Griffith.

Colophon

This book is set in Palatino, an old-style serif typeface designed by the German typographer Hermann Zapf; and also in **Comic Sans**, by typographer Vincent Connare, for the Microsoft Corporation. It was designed by Steve Chappell and printed and bound by Worzalla Printing.

Paul Buhle has published more than forty volumes on popular culture, film, and social movements. He was until his retirement a senior lecturer at Brown University, and is a Distinguished Lecturer for the American Studies Association and the Organization of American History. His previous comics include adaptations of Howard Zinn's and Studs Terkel's work, several biographies, and histories of the Beat Generation. He now lives in Madison.

Some of the books that Paul Buhle has authored or edited are:

C.L.R. James: The Artist as Revolutionary

Encyclopedia of the American Left
(with Mari Jo Buhle and Dan Georgakas)

Wobblies! A Graphic History of the Industrial Workers of the World
(with Nicole Schulman)

Students for a Democratic Society: A Graphic History
(with Harvey Pekar and Gary Dumm)

History and the New Left: Madison, Wisconsin, 1950-70

A People's History of American Empire
(with Howard Zinn, Mike Konopacki, and Dave Wagner)

Jews and American Comics

The Art of Harvey Kurtzman
(with Denis Kitchen)